COMMUNICATION IN THE WORKPLACE

Everything You Need To Know About
Effective Communication Strategies At
Work To Be A Better Leader

SHIRLEY COLE

Copyright 2019 © Shirley Cole

All rights reserved.

No part of this guide may be reproduced in any form without permission in writing from the publisher except in the case of review.

Legal & Disclaimer

The following document is reproduced below with the goal of providing information that is as accurate and reliable as possible.

This declaration is deemed fair and valid by both the American Bar Association and the Committee of Publishers Association and is legally binding throughout the United States.

Furthermore, the transmission, duplication or reproduction of any of the following work including specific information will be considered an illegal act irrespective of if it is done electronically or in print. This extends to creating a secondary or tertiary copy of the work or a recorded copy and is only allowed with an express written consent from the Publisher. All additional right reserved.

The information in the following pages is broadly considered to be a truthful and accurate account of facts, and as such any inattention, use or misuse of the information in question by the reader will render any resulting actions solely under their purview. There are no scenarios in which the publisher or the original author of this work can be in any fashion deemed liable for any hardship or damages that may befall them after undertaking information described herein.

Additionally, the information in the following pages is intended only for informational purposes and should thus be thought of as universal. As befitting its nature, it is presented without assurance regarding its prolonged validity or interim quality. Trademarks that are mentioned are done without written consent and can in no way be considered an endorsement from the trademark holder.

Table of Contents

Introduction 6

Chapter One: The Incredible Power of Effective Communication in The Workplace 14

Chapter Two: How to Develop Effective and Persuasive Communication Skills at Work 48

Chapter Three: How to Effectively Handle Difficult Situations and People in the Workplace 126

Chapter Four: How to Be The Most Effective Leader You Can Be 161

Chapter Five: The Most Common Communication Mistakes and How to Avoid Them 190

Chapter Six: Expert Tips and Tricks for Effective Communication in The Workplace 199

Bonus Chapter: How to Become a Master at Public Speaking 210

Final Words 219

Introduction

Communication is at the core of every human relationship. We all communicate with each other in some form or another, every day. Communication in the workplace can be especially tricky. The way in which you communicate with other individuals in your workplace or your business, can go a long way in how others perceive you and thus relate to you. Learning to effectively communicate isn't just about resolving conflict in the workplace. Effective communication also plays a large contributing factor in your relationships with clients, the business's profitability, employee engagement and retention and how effectively a team can function together.

Effective communication is a skill that each one of us has the power to master. As an employee, you should make an effort to learn how to effectively communicate, not just for others' benefit, but for yourself as well. In this book you will learn proven strategies on how to effectively communicate with your coworkers or employees and be able to express your message without any confusion or frustration. Successful businesses are built on healthy working relationships and effective communication. As an employee or business owner, you have the power to contribute to the success of the business by honing your communication skills (Bosworth, 2019). Your own personal communication style has an influence on other individuals and can be used to create thriving business relationships. Effective communication in the workplace isn't just about being able to accurately express your ideas or about getting your point across, it is so much more than that. It also goes far beyond just resolving conflict or creating a positive team environment. Being able to effectively communicate in the workplace is essential to client relationships, the company's culture, your sales process, building a better team environment and employee engagement. Building an effective communication strategy within the workplace promotes innovation, removes cultural barriers, helps to mitigate conflict and creates transparency, which helps to promote inclusivity.

But why should you listen to anything I have to say about mastering effective communication in the workplace?

Hi, my name is Shirley Cole and I am a professional management and communications consultant. Over the years, I have helped many executives and organizations achieve a greater impact by teaching them how to focus on the needs of their employees through understanding their communication channels. In addition to this, I also give lectures and seminars all over the world to global organizations which focus on creating solutions for communication problems within team settings. I take great joy in helping to transform organizations using the principles I have outlined in this book.

A lack of effective communication in the workplace can cause a lot of different issues. Someone might drop the ball on an important client project due to a miscommunication. Team members might butt heads due to ineffective communication or employees may not fully understand the company culture. When you can effectively communicate with your team members and coworkers, all of these issues can be avoided.

There is a common thread that I see when I work with organizations, no matter the size or type of industry. The company's workforce is very competent and hard-working, however, they often carry around pervasive bad communication habits which lead to drama, anger, mistrust and low morale. This can happen within that individual team and carry over into other departments. It is my goal in this book to share my vast knowledge on how to overcome personality and communication issues so that you (as an employee or employer) can work towards creating a more comfortable and productive working environment. My clients regularly praise me for positively changing their work processes and helping them to create connections that are authentic, energizing and rewarding with both their colleagues and customers through skillful conversations.

The purpose of this book is to show you how to improve your workplace relations by using effective communication strategies. This can easily be done by learning your coworkers' language of appreciation. By outlining exactly how to effectively communicate authentic messages of appreciation and encouragement to employees, coworkers and leaders; this book will provide you with the tools to create a more positive workplace, improve staff morale and increase employee engagement. Many issues within the workplace stem from the question of how to make people feel appreciated. This comprehensive guide to interpersonal communication will provide you with the tools to do just that, by creating a better environment for production, thriving client relationships, high employee engagement and continual team development.

Here is just a small snapshot of the workplace communication strategies that I have included in this book:

- The psychology behind being able to effectively communicate at work.
- How to become a better listener in the workplace.
- The barriers to effective communication in the workplace and how to overcome them.
- Clarifying your values, finding your voice, and effective goal setting.
- How to correctly give and receive criticism.
- The importance of positivity in the workplace.
- Common communication mistakes and how to avoid them.
- How to deal with difficult people or bosses.
- Becoming a master at public speaking.
- Managing difficult conversations and time wasters.
- Asking questions that get results.
- Effective communication using body language, verbal and non-verbal skills.

You could try and piece this all together yourself by reading websites and other books that only give you bits and pieces. However, do you really have the time for all that? This is the most comprehensive book that you will find that will give you the exact tools you need in order to create a thriving work environment where everyone appreciates and actually understands one another.

Don't wait for a lack of communication to cripple your client relationships or misunderstandings to muddle your sales process. Whether you work in a cubicle, a factory or within a virtual team, learning effective communication strategies will make a world of difference in your professional life. If you want to create crystal clear workplace communication processes, then keep reading!

Chapter One: The Incredible Power of Effective Communication in The Workplace

So often in the workplace, we send quick emails and memos to one another in order to communicate (sometimes very vital) information. However, there is a major disadvantage to this. Messages can be misinterpreted or misunderstood, which then causes a breakdown in the communication processes. The sole use of technology - such as emails or instant messaging - when communicating within the workplace removes essential information that can be gained through the use of body language and tone of voice.

What Is Effective Communication In The Workplace?

Being able to effectively communicate within the workplace takes place through a series of verbal and non-verbal processes to promote professional relationships. In order to promote effective communication within the workplace, you must first take a look at and identify any potential barriers before moving on.

There are many, many barriers to effective

communication in the workplace. Some of the most common include interrupting others or interruptions from others, inattentive listening, a failure to properly read body language and other non-verbal cues, gender differences (yes, men and women communicate differently), not getting the whole story or jumping to conclusions and inappropriate reactions (both verbally and non-verbally) to others (Effectivecommunicationadvice.com, 2019). In order to be a more effective communicator in the workplace, there are several things that you can do:

- Ensure that your body language and what you are saying match up.
- Being aware of gender differences in communication styles and how to effectively handle them.
- Having an understanding of cultural differences and how to work with many

different types of people.
- Not relying so much on technology and communicating in person.
- Be able to give and receive constructive criticism
- Keeping emotions out of the equation.

When you work to create effective communication within the workplace it creates positivity and an enjoyable environment for you and those around you. This can also help to decrease workplace stress while increasing productivity and overall employee morale.

The Psychology Behind Effective Communication in The Workplace

Your brain reacts to any stimuli that it encounters (Chadwick, 2014). When you experience stress, fear, anxiety, happiness, satisfaction and joy, your brain takes those emotions and it processes them through reactions from the limbic system (Moawad, 2017). When our brains experience a negative emotion like stress, this then has a negative knock-on effect on our brains and our emotional wellbeing. Your focus becomes decreased, your ability to concentrate becomes inhibited and your general cognitive abilities are reduced. This can have many side effects in the workplace. If you are not able to focus, you may misunderstand a direction or make a simple mistake that could drastically affect some other areas of the work.

Positive emotions have just the opposite effect on the brain. When you are experiencing positive emotions and positivity in the workplace, you are more likely to be able to focus better and will be able to perform better on tasks that are cognitively demanding, such as creative thinking, cognitive flexibility and faster processing of information.

When an employee is being yelled at or they are becoming overly stressed out about something, this puts them into the flight, fight or freeze mode. You see, your brain can not process whether or not a threat is real or perceived. This is due to the production of cortisol, also known as the stress hormone. When you are experiencing stress, no matter if it is real or perceived, you produce cortisol. So if your boss is screaming at you or you are freaking out over a mistake, your brain processes this the same way as if you were being chased by a tiger. This triggers physiological responses that take energy away from your prefrontal cortex, which helps us to think logically and rationally. So, if your prefrontal cortex is not able to process things correctly, it makes it very difficult to be productive at work.

Why You Need Effective Communication in The Workplace

There are so many reasons to advocate for healthy and positive communication in the workplace. Here are some of the core reasons to promote effective communication at work (Richason, 2017):

- It creates a healthy working environment.
- Helps to remove cultural barriers.
- An increase in bottom-line profits.
- Mitigates conflicts.
- Increases employee engagement.
- Fosters a sense of teamwork.
- Promotes innovation.
- Boosts customer service and satisfaction.
- Increases employee retention.
- Provides transparency within the organization.
- Increased employee productivity.

With all of these benefits, it's no wonder that communication in the workplace is a hot topic.

What Is Internal And External Communication?

There are two basic categories of communication; internal and external (Webb, 2017). Internal communication focuses on the communication between the employee and the company, whereas external communication focuses on the communication outward to customers, clients, vendors or contractors.

Each of these different kinds of communication is handled differently. Internal communications are used to inform, motivate and/or provide feedback to employees. The various forms of internal communications can include internal emails, memos, phone calls, face to face meetings and instant messages. What you say and how you communicate with internal employees is generally different than when you communicate with someone external from the company.

External communications generally take place with customers and other "employees" that are external to the company like vendors or contractors. While external communications can include many of the same types of communications as internal, there are some differences. Your company's website, social media, email newsletter, advertising and so on are all different ways that your company can communicate externally. When your employees communicate via phone, email, text or instant messaging to your customers, this is an external communication.

While each of these types of communications is different, the basic principles behind effective communication can be used for all types, both external and internal.

The Barriers That Prohibit Effective Communication In The Workplace

There is a wide variety of factors that can inhibit effective communication in the workplace; gender, cultural barriers, tone and body language, your brains being hijacked by your emotions, external noise, emotions, and so much more (Zambas, 2019).

First, let's talk about gender. This is a really big one that people might not fully realize is such a barrier to effective communication, particularly in the workplace. Generally speaking, when a woman runs into an issue, she needs to talk it out to help her process the problem and will come to her own solution. This is not her trying to complain but rather work out the problem while talking aloud about it. She is not necessarily seeking a solution to the problem from an external source but rather using what she already has to put together a solution. Men generally think logically and if they need to solve a problem will often seclude themselves while processing the issue at hand. This can create communication barriers in the workplace, just simply because of different genders conversing with each other.

For the most part, men are problem solvers. If a woman comes to them to discuss an issue, he will tend to look for a solution and offer it to them. Generally, if a woman goes to another woman to discuss a problem, she may ask her colleague open-ended questions to help her figure out the solution on her own. If a woman needs to collaborate with a man on something, she should give him explicit instructions as to what needs to be done and what she is expecting.

Men and women also communicate differently

with their body language. They can make the same gestures but it will mean two completely different things. A head nod for example. When a woman nods her head she does that as a sign that she is listening; when a man does it, he does it as a sign of agreement (Jenkins, 2018). So you can see how something as simple as a head nod can cause a miscommunication between colleagues.

Cultural barriers can also cause a lack of effective communication in the workplace. Cultural communication barriers can be present when working with colleagues for whom English is their second language and the uses of certain gestures (Gottfried, 2018); such as shaking hands or bowing (Dabbah, 2018). Where one culture might use handshakes to greet one another, another culture will use a bow, which can quickly cause miscommunication. Cultural miscommunications can be internal or external.

For example, if a company makes and sells products or services geared toward a specific culture but they do not fully understand it, their message might not come across as intended.

Tone and body language can also be very large barriers to effective workplace communication. The actual words you say in a conversation only account for about 7% of your overall communication. This leaves a lot of room for miscommunication from body language and overall tone. Having your arms crossed while in a conversation with someone shows that you are being closed off, whereas having your arms relaxed at your sides (or talking with your hands) shows that you are open to the conversation and are taking in the information. If you are sitting and speaking with someone, leaning in towards them with your body and feet facing them shows that you are engaged in the conversation. If, on the other hand, you are leaning back in your chair with your body turned or feet facing the door, then this shows that you are not engaged in the conversation and may even signal that you want to get up and leave.

Internal and external noise can also be a very large barrier to effective communication. External noise can include working in a very loud factory; it might be very difficult to effectively speak with someone so they can fully hear and understand everything you are saying to them due to the environmental noises. Internal noise could be trying to listen at a meeting but you are thinking about the argument that you had with your spouse earlier that day instead.

We previously talked about the psychology of effective workplace communication and how your brain plays a role in how well you can communicate with your colleagues. If you are experiencing some kind of internal or external stressor, your physiological responses are going to hijack your brain and cause you to enter the flight, fight or freeze response.

The Importance of A Positive Mindset In The Workplace

The importance of positivity in the workplace cannot be stressed enough. Positivity has been tied to every aspect of success within the workplace such as profit, productivity and satisfaction. Everyone in the workplace can benefit from positivity, both the employer and the employees.

Employers are all about their bottom line and how employees can make them more profitable. Positivity in the workplace increases productivity, thus increasing overall profits. Some of the largest, most profitable companies in the world have figured out that if they keep their employees happy, engaged and positive, their bottom line increases. There is a simple reasoning behind this correlation. Happier employees translate into happier customers. Happier customers tend to buy more and have greater loyalty to the company and become repeat customers and refer friends and family to the company.

A positive environment also leads to a higher retention of a company's good employees. The number one reason that people leave a position or a workplace is that it is in some way negative. It might be a toxic or caustic work environment, somehow negative. It doesn't really matter what they are getting paid; if the work environment is negative, they don't want to work there. Employee retention is highly affected by how positive or negative the work environment is.

There are two aspects of positivity in the workplace; evaluation and creation. If you are a leader or manager of some kind within your workplace, you are likely at some point going to have to evaluate your employees' or team's performance. While it might be easy to see what they could be doing better, this can take a negative overtone. When employees feel that they can never please their employer, that will likely hit their morale. It will only benefit your team if you provide them with a positive evaluation. Let them know that they are doing a good job and you are proud of the work and their commitment to that work. Of course, there are some aspects that they could improve upon, but that is not the focus here. The focus of the evaluation process is to provide your employees with positive feedback. Leave out the *"but!"* Don't go in evaluating your employees like, *"you guys are doing good, but..."* - this is just going to ruin all of the good things that you just said.

While positive evaluation is going to make your team feel great about themselves, you are not staying there. As a manager or leader, give your evaluation, pause and let your employees revel in the positive energy that you have just created, then move on. While your team might be doing well, it is likely that there is some area for improvement that they could be focusing on. When the team focuses on the things they are not excelling at, that creates anxiety. However, when you imagine what you have is going to be better than what you already have, that creates a lot of positive energy and hope within the team. There is a delicate balance between giving a positive evaluation and moving forward to create something even better. When you are communicating with your employees, start with a positive evaluation, move onto the creation of something better and always end on a positive note of encouragement!

How does having a positive work environment benefit the employee? Unless you are completely retired, you are either an employee or self-employed (and might employ other people). If you are an employee, the most obvious benefit of a positive work environment is that you, as the employee, get to be happy. I mean, what is really our most commonly shared goal in life? To be happy! When you look at people's goals, it really doesn't matter what it is, to be their own boss, to make more money, to travel the world, this all leads back to happiness and the experience of happiness. When you are in a work environment that is a positive one, you are going to be happier.

Other benefits to employees of positivity in the workplace are increased job satisfaction, employee retention, productivity, which can also lead to the potential for new opportunities and increases in wage or salary. You might be truly amazed as to how an increase in your own positivity, as an employee, can lead to opportunities both within and outside of the organization. When managers and leaders of an organization continue to see positivity and high levels of production from employees, they want to keep them around and they want to reward them. You might even be presented with opportunities you did not even realize you had available to you.

You see, there is a little secret about positivity

that I am going to share with you. It is contagious! When you are positive within one area of your life, it is going to carry over into other areas of your life, such as your love life, your parenting, your finances, and so on.

The Transformative Power of Good Communication In The Workplace

There is a real power to learning how to effectively communicate in the workplace. Effective communication can mitigate conflict, increase employee engagement and create better client relationships while also resulting in a more productive and talented workforce.

Conflict within the workplace results from misunderstandings or feeling misunderstood, not understanding how to communicate with others effectively or when someone feels they are being disrespected or their emotional needs are not being met. When you learn and implement effective communication strategies, misunderstandings can be avoided, you are able to effectively communicate with others and your colleagues will feel respected and that their emotional needs are being met.

Employees become more engaged in the workplace using good communication through connecting with people (Page, 2019). When employees understand what is asked of them, they are able to become aligned with the company's goals and objectives while establishing good communication with their team members. There are several areas in which effective communication can help to improve overall employee engagement. As an employer, it gives you the tools to fully understand the goals and needs of your employees. It gives you the information you need to understand your employees' goals and needs. It provides a better connection and understanding with your employees' skills and talents that you may not have otherwise noticed. It will also give you the ability to cultivate those talents while being cohesive with the company's goals and values. It can improve your connections with coworkers and colleagues to create a more satisfying and positive working environment, as well as build a better relationship with leaders and managers within the organization.

Having effective communication in the workplace also creates a better relationship with clients and customers. Customer and client relationships are at the core of all organizations. Client-facing employees can make or break an organization and be the difference between a satisfied or disgruntled customer. When employees understand how to effectively communicate with customers, it helps them to understand the customer's needs and help the customer to feel understood. It also enables staff to resolve and mitigate any conflicts the customer might have. Effective communication can also help the employee to present information to the customer in a new way that will help the customer to be more receptive.

Furthermore, the workplace will become more productive and increase its talent when it has effective communications strategies in place. When employees are engaged at work they are more productive. When employees are productive and engaged, this helps the leadership team to understand their employees' talents and skills. Employees also become more committed to their workplace and organizations can expect a higher level of buy-in from their employees. Workplaces that focus on effective communication help to foster innovation and creative thought as employees feel safe to express their ideas to their leadership team. This also helps employees to take ownership of their projects and challenges while encouraging creative brainstorming. Leaders will then take notice and use these new found creative brainstorming processes and innovation to build more strategic teams based on employees' strengths.

When applying for jobs, effective communication skills can help to set people apart from other applicants. Ineffective communication in the workplace will ultimately lead to unmotivated employees and employees questioning their ability and confidence within the organization. When there is consistent and effective communication in the workplace, the company is equipped for growth. Growing a company requires both internal and external communication. The company must ensure they are delivering a consistent message externally to their clients and customers.

There are several ways to improve communication within your organization to ensure that employees and the organization are reaching their full potential. You should establish clearlier defined goals and expectations. The leadership team needs to ensure that the goals and expectations for their employees are clear and achievable. They also need to make sure that all of their employees are aware of and understand the objectives of the project as well as the department and organization as a whole. Whatever the message is that is being delivered, it should be clear and your intended audience should easily be able to understand it. When speaking to your intended audience you should always remember to speak politely and plainly so that your message is delivered without offense or confusion.

You must also consider which medium you are choosing to deliver your message through.

While, more often than not, face to face communication is preferred, it is not always possible. This can be especially true for virtual teams. When you have to send a message via print or virtually, read it aloud to ensure that it comes across as you are intending it to. In a professional setting, you should avoid the use of emojis or overly expressive text and write in a neutral font and tone.

It is best to keep everyone involved in the process and projects by use of frequent updates and progress reports. This, again, is especially important when working with a remote team. Keeping everyone involved and the lines of communication open will help to ensure that everyone is on the same page while having a less likely chance that miscommunications will occur.

Listening is just as important (if not more important) in the workplace as talking. When you are in a conversation with someone, be engaged with your listening and show empathy. Communicating with someone is a two-way street. The company and the employee will thrive when dialog is encouraged and respect is shown.

While good communication might come easily and even naturally to some, it can be difficult for others to accurately express how they are feeling or the message they are trying to get across. A lack of effective communication can lead to conflict and fundamental errors that could ultimately be avoided if those communicating just understood the message. Just as you can experience miscommunications outside of the workplace, they can happen equally easily within the workplace. It has been shown that 70% of mistakes in businesses are due to a lack of effective communication (Allan, 2019).

Efficiency also increases in the workplace when

employees practice good communication. When poor communication happens, efficiency is compromised in addition to the quality of work. On the other hand, when instructions are clear and concise, this eliminates any need to clarify or correct any issues that might arise. If you happen to be an effective communicator but those around you are not so great, make sure you are asking the right questions to get the answers and clarification that you need in order to proceed without confusion.

When there is good communication in the workplace, employee loyalty increases. Employees feel comfortable discussing issues that might arise and feel free to express their ideas with their leadership team. This helps to build trust and loyalty among team members and the management team. This also eliminates the need for management to micromanage employees and gives them more autonomy within their roles.

Chapter Summary

Technology can greatly inhibit effective communication within the workplace. We send quick emails and memos thinking that our point will get across or our message will be effectively communicated, but this is not always true. Technology alone can not express how we are feeling and lacks non-verbal cues, which can lead to misunderstandings and misinterpretations of the message you were trying to send.

Before you are able to effectively communicate in the workplace, you first need to identify and be able to move past any potential barriers. This can include gender biases, stereotypes and cultural barriers in order to effectively communicate with your colleagues and/or employees. Here are some of the most common barriers to communication in the workplace:

- Gender differences.
- Inattentive listening.
- A miscommunication in body language.
- Not getting the whole story and or jumping to conclusions.
- Inappropriate verbal and non-verbal reactions.
- A negative outlook.

You must understand that when it comes to stress in the workplace or any other area of life, our brains can not perceive whether or not a threat is real or perceived. Therefore your brain is not able to determine if the stress you are experiencing is real or not real.

There are many reasons why you need effective communication in the workplace, such as increasing bottom-line profits and providing transparency within the organization. You can ensure that you are promoting effective communication in the workplace both internally and externally through recognizing and removing gender and cultural barriers, being aware of both verbal and nonverbal communication and minimizing noise.

Positive communication in the workplace is also very important. The more positive the employee, the more productive they are, which then leads to higher profits. Leaders should always ensure that they are providing their workforce with positive feedback.

There is a real power to mastering effective communication in the workplace. It helps to stomp out conflict, increase employee engagement, build and maintain healthier client relationships and results in a happier and more productive workforce.

In the next chapter, you will learn how to

develop effective and persuasive communication skills in the workplace.

Chapter Two:
How to Develop Effective and Persuasive Communication Skills at Work

Now that we have outlined why you should learn to effectively communicate in the workplace, it is time to outline exactly HOW. This includes everything from verbal and non-verbal communication including body language and being aware of your facial expressions. Now is the time to become a better listener at work and learn how to explain what you are trying to communicate to your colleagues. As a team member in your workplace, you need to learn to become an inclusive communicator and be able to communicate with people from all different backgrounds and all different levels of management.

It is also beneficial to learn persuasive techniques in order to persuade team members and your leadership team to your points of view. These techniques can be used if you have found a better, more efficient way of doing things but others are still stuck in the *"we have always done it this way,"* mentality. Whether you are a leader or member of management in your workplace or are a "low-level" employee, you should be equipped with the skills to both give and receive criticism and be able to share meaningful feedback in a tactful and positive manner.

Your written communications can also have a large effect on how well you communicate with your coworkers. When you speak with someone about an issue or a project, are you asking the right questions to get to the bottom of things or clarify your role? In this chapter, we are going to cover what kinds of questions to ask to get the information that you desire, as well as the secrets to being a proactive communicator, and how to report professionally.

Sending Messages: Verbal and Non-Verbal Communication Skills

There are two main types of communication that humans use; verbal and non-verbal. Each of them sends messages to another party (Surbhi 2019). Verbal communication includes both writing and speaking. It is the words that you say and the words that you write. Non-verbal communication includes everything else and accounts for about 90% of your overall communication. Non-verbal communication includes body language, facial expressions and even sign language (Frost, 2016). The chances of a miscommunication are much greater with non-verbal language than with verbal language.

Verbal communication, which is what you are currently experiencing reading this book, is the most effective form of communication and it can be used to quickly and easily transmit information and or feedback. The communication can be oral, such as a face-to-face conversation, phone calls, lectures, videos and seminars or written, which includes email, text messages, handwritten or typed letters, and so on.

Within the realms of verbal communication, there is also formal and informal. It is likely that most of the communication that you do while at work, will be formal. Formal communication follows a predefined channel in order for the sender to get the information to the receiver. The opposite is true for informal communication: the sender and receiver do not follow any kind of predetermined outline. A work memo would be considered a formal communication, while an example of informal could be a quick text to your coworkers.

Non-verbal communication is something else entirely. There are many, many different types of non-verbal communication. There is chronemics, which is the punctuality and the speed at which the person is speaking. Have you ever met someone who talked really fast about something? What was your impression? Most likely you thought that person was excited about what they were talking about. Although there are many other factors that come into play. Such as the vocalics; this is the volume, tone and pitch of someone's voice. If someone is talking very loudly, they could be upset or just be trying to talk over other environmental noise.

Then we move into the external kinds of non-verbal communication. Haptics is the use of touch when someone is communicating, as a way for them to express their emotions and feelings. This would be something like rubbing someone's arm as you are verbally trying to comfort them. Kinesics is the body language, gestures, posture and facial expressions that a person uses while communicating (more on that soon). The distance at which someone places themselves when communicating to others is known as proxemics. This generally includes different amounts of space for intimate, personal, social and public relationships. People can also communicate non-verbally through their artifacts; this includes the way they dress, their accessories or lifestyle. You are likely to communicate to someone differently (especially with your non-verbal language) if they are wearing a suit than if they are wearing workout clothes.

How To Use and Understand Body Language

Your body language says a lot about who you are and sends a lot of signals to your fellow coworkers. We all do our best to make a good impression on those we work with by carefully choosing our words, but you might not realize how big a stake in your communication that your body language contributes. Without even realizing it, you might be sabotaging your best efforts with your colleagues and clients just by how you are communicating with your body language. You can use body language in the workplace to improve your communication and help to make a positive impression. The use of body language can be intentional or completely unconscious. Your body language has a very strong influence on how other people perceive you. Some examples of poor body language include rolling your eyes, slouching or folding your arms in front of you. When you realize how your body language is received and perceived by others this can help you to communicate more effectively.

A very effective use of body language in the workplace is to maintain eye contact while speaking to someone. When you maintain eye contact while you are speaking to someone or they are speaking to you, this portrays that you are showing interest, paying attention, that you feel confident and are communicating honestly. If you are speaking to someone and you don't maintain eye contact with them, they may feel that you are being dishonest. If someone is speaking to you and you avert your gaze, they may feel that you are not paying attention to them. Posture is also a very useful body language tool. When you slouch or slump in your chair, others will think that you are uninterested in what is going on. When you maintain an erect posture, it shows your attentiveness and engagement in the conversation or communication. If you are sitting and speaking to someone you should lean towards them slightly rather than lean back in your chair. This is another way to show engagement and that you are paying attention to what they are saying.

It is important to be aware of your own body language but also the body language of others around you. When you are speaking with a person or listening to them, be aware of their body language and how they move when they are talking. Other people's body language can help you to determine the kind of message that they are trying to deliver. Are they lacking confidence? If an employee is lacking confidence in a particular area, perhaps they could use additional training or support to help them thrive. If you sense that they are lacking in certain areas, try to nicely call them out on it without making them feel uncomfortable. Saying something as simple as, *"Hey [name], do you recall when we spoke about [topic], I got the sense that you are lacking confidence in [task], how can I help you become more confident in that area?"* Saying it this way lets your colleague know that you are not trying to be rude but to help them reach their full potential.

You can also use the skill of reading people's body language when you are giving a presentation or lecture. Being able to effectively gauge the body language of your audience will help you to determine how your message is being received. You should easily be able to tell how engaged your audience is by their eye contact, posture and other body movements. If your audience is lacking eye contact, tend to be fidgeting a lot with pens or phones and are slouching and leaning back in their chairs, they are probably disengaged with the message you are trying to send.

If an employee disagrees with the speakers' message, they will use their body language to signal that as well. When people feel threatened or unsafe in some way - this can even just be a simple disagreement in a message they are receiving - they will become closed off. Their body language might include turning their feet or whole body away from you, crossing their arms or leaning back in their chairs. Pay close attention, if you see this happening, try and open up the discussion to see if you can figure out what your audience disagrees with you on. Ask them for solutions to the issues. While, with a little practice, you can understand your colleagues' body language and should be able to recognize how they are feeling, misinterpreting body language can have a drastically different effect. When body language is misinterpreted, that can lead to friction, conflict and misunderstandings of all kinds. The likelihood of communication misunderstandings only increases as a workplace becomes more diverse and cultural differences might come into play. If you are communicating with someone in your workplace and they seem to be showing negative body language, that could mean they are frustrated, bored or being dishonest. You should respond before you react. Reacting to body language will only lead to further friction and conflict. Do your best to investigate their body language and feelings further. Ask your colleague additional questions that could shed some light on their body language and how they are feeling.

There is an upside to all of this though, the longer you work with someone, the more you get to know their body language and be able to read their body language becomes easier over time.

Here are some of the body language mistakes that you are making at work that you might not even realize:

- Having bad posture or slouching.
- Fidgeting.
- Having a tense expression on your face.
- Being too casual.
- Not making eye contact or looking down.
- Crossing your arms.
- Standing too close to people.

It takes some time to become aware of your body language, how your body language affects other people and to be able to understand other's body language. Just as with any other skill, the more you practice it the better you will become at it. So when you are in conversation with someone, pay attention to how they are using their body and how they are responding to your body language.

How to Become Aware of Your Facial Expressions

Your facial expressions also play into your body language and how people perceive you. Your facial expression is your first impression when meeting others; this includes customers, colleagues and clients. The expressions that you make with your face are inherently used for social cues and to give others around you clues as to how you are feeling. Your facial expression can affect the trajectory of the conversation or social interaction (Russell, 2015). Even if you don't mean to, your facial expressions can give away your feelings and this can lead to people perceiving you in a certain light in the workplace. Here are three situations that you might find yourself in where your facial expressions are giving away more than you want them to.

When you greet someone at work that you do not like. When you don't like someone and are in their presence, you may often express this through a scowl on your face. This can be detrimental to your working relationships as it shows that person and others around you that you do not like that individual. When you are greeting someone that you don't like, trying to greet them with a slight smile will always leave a better impression than a scowl or frown.

Unforeseen circumstances in your workload can also show on your facial expressions. This can happen when you get an increase in your workload; your facial expression might indicate that you feel that you can not handle it, with a furrowed brow or pout on your face. Ensure that your facial expressions don't indicate to your other colleagues that you feel you are incapable of the hard work you are being asked to do.

Generally, you smile when you are happy, and often when you receive a compliment, however, this facial expression comes off differently when you are in the workplace. A smile when you receive a compliment can make you come across as smug, and you don't want this! When you receive a compliment on something you did well on, just say *"thank you,"* give a polite nod and give a slight smile to acknowledge the positive comment you received. You don't want to seem like you have a big ego when you give a big smile showing all of your teeth; gloating doesn't go over very well in the workplace.

That's not to say that you should try and avoid showing facial expressions at work, it simply means that you should be aware of the facial expression that you are showing and how they can be perceived by those around you.

The Keys to Becoming a Better Listener at Work

Being a good listener at work can be difficult sometimes, especially if there is a lot of environmental noise. There are a few key things that you can do to practice better listening skills at work. The easiest is being quiet and letting the other person speak without trying to think of what you are going to say to them right away. Secondly, if you are engaging in a two-way conversation, repeat back to that person what you heard them say. *"So what I am hearing you say is [this], did I get that correct?"* Not only does this validate to the sender of the message that you are paying attention and actually listening to them, it also helps to eliminate any misunderstandings.

Many people are not very good listeners. All too

often people might hear what someone is saying but they are not truly listening; if you are a parent, you know this well. People also listen to see when they can start talking. You can learn a lot from a person just by listening to them and letting them talk. Keep this in mind; we have one mouth and two ears, therefore we should listen twice as much as we talk.

Becoming a better listener can help you to deepen your relationship to the person you are communicating with (Edberg, 2019). This works both in the workplace and in your personal life. People often have a difficult time listening because they feel that they don't personally gain anything from it. When you truly listen to someone, it is likely that they will listen better to you as well. The main point of listening is to understand what the person is trying to communicate to you.

Listening to someone speak is like playing a

game of memory. When you are trying to remember what someone is saying, try and process the information like you have to tell someone else about it later. Even if you don't actually have to repeat the information, this can be very helpful in recalling information from the conversation. This will help you to be more alert and even ask more questions to help you understand what the person is trying to communicate to you. This should also help you to focus more on what the person is saying and to stop thinking so much about what you are going to say next.

Did you know your eyes can help you to become a better listener? Maintaining eye contact during a conversation can help you to focus on what the other person is saying, thus helping you to retain more information. If you have issues or feel weird about staring someone in the eyes, look directly at the center of their nose, they will never know the difference.

Cut out technological distractions. This is a BIG one! It is very difficult to be able to effectively listen to someone when you are scrolling through your phone or on your computer. This can lead to misunderstanding what the other person is saying or completely missing points of the conversation. When you are on your phone or computer it also makes the other person feel as though you are not listening to them.

You can let the other person know you are listening by summarizing what they said. When you are able to summarize what was said this lets them know that you were listening and that you have understood what was said. This also helps to clear up any potential misunderstandings that might otherwise occur.

While it would be great if you could read people's

minds to mitigate any misunderstandings, you cannot. You can, however, ask questions to clarify what is being said. Try and stick to open-ended questions to gain a further understanding of what they are trying to communicate to you. Asking open-ended questions also encourages them to open up and explore what they are saying and dive more in-depth into the conversation.

You can also be a better listener when you are prepared to listen. If you know that you are going into a long meeting that could potentially put you to sleep, make sure you are mentally and physically prepared to listen. It is difficult enough to listen, much less understand the message someone is trying to get across when you are falling asleep or feeling foggy. In order to get your mind working and prepared for an intake of information, get some fresh air! You can do this by opening a window in your office (if you have any) or going for a short walk outside. You can also just do a bit of exercise to get your blood flowing to your brain.

When you listen, you just need to listen. Don't think about adding your input, interrupting the sender or jumping to solutions or conclusions. Just try and be present in the moment and fully listen to understand what the sender is saying. Sometimes when people are talking, all they really need is someone to listen to them so that they can vent or work out their own issues.

If for whatever reason you are not able to give someone your full attention and listen to them, be honest about it. Let them know that you are too tired, busy or distracted at this point to hold a valuable conversation and ask them if it is possible to continue it later. Set a time that you feel that you will both be able to have a conversation with minimal noise interference.

How to Become a Better Communicator at Work Through Better Explanation

You can't make everyone be a more effective communicator. You can do your best, however, to make sure you are explaining things to the best of your ability. We talked quite a bit earlier about how your body language has a very large effect on how your colleagues perceive you at work. Body language is one area you can focus on to help you better explain the message you are trying to get across. Make sure that the words that you are saying and the message that your body language and your tone of voice are giving off are all cohesive. Saying that you are excited to start on a new project while having a somber tone and a frown sends conflicting messages.

Asking questions in a conversation goes both ways. When you are speaking with someone or an audience, ask them periodically if they understand or if something needs more explanation. Checking in with people to ensure that they are understanding what you are communicating will also help you to sharpen your explanation skills.

Diversified Work Environments: How to Become a More Inclusive Communicator

First of all, I would like to address what inclusive communication actually is. It's unfortunate that this still happens, but discrimination in the workplace is still very prevalent today, particularly between men and women. While women make up about 50% of the workforce, there are less than 15% that hold executive positions (Warner, 2019). While you should already be aware that men and women communicate differently, the discrimination that occurs is often unconscious as it is inadvertently reinforced in everyday conversations. Inclusive communication is a communication style that transcends gender and cultural biases so that each party understands and is understood.

Generally speaking, women are better at bringing a sense of personal connection to the workplace. Workplaces can all too often be stoggy and mechanical. People are going to perform their tasks better when they feel appreciated and heard by their leadership team. Leaders within the organization, whether male or female, should not be afraid of vulnerability, attention or authenticity.

The modern definition of gender is drastically different than the archaic one that most people understand. As employees or employers, we all need to move past that antiquated vision of what gender binary is and include a broader range of identities and genders within the workplace. We can work to overcome gender gaps and unconscious biases through acknowledgment and admission of how these biases have influenced our behaviors, thoughts and feelings.

You must also adjust your speaking and listening styles to be less definitive. While people might be able to easily express facts and ideas, it might be more difficult for them to express their feelings or values. When in conversation, acknowledge the fact or idea and listen for the feelings and values behind it. Paraphrase what your colleague said to you and seek to understand the true meaning behind it.

Along with being able to recognize your own gender biases, you should also be able to recognize and allow for different styles of communication. This is especially crucial for leaders within the organization, regardless of their gender identification. Leaders should work towards maintaining a style of communication that is open and allows for unique perspectives.

In order to become an inclusive and effective communicator, you need to be able to stop talking and genuinely engage with the people you are communicating with. Generally speaking, at work, men speak freely and do not wait for an invitation to talk, whereas women generally wait for a request of their input. Male leaders could then benefit from pausing before talking and making an attempt to reach out to their female counterparts asking for their input, opinions and ideas. This will result in a more productive and diverse work environment. Furthermore, male leaders need to work towards building strong relationships with every member of their team.

As an employee or a leader, you must move past any preconceived notions and stereotypical responses that you carry internally and work to remove your limiting beliefs. Do your best to be open to the person you are having a conversation with, both internally and externally. Focus on building relationships and understanding each other's needs and building trust within your team.

How to Get People to Agree With You: Putting Together an Effective and Persuasive Message

Every day in your workplace you put together messages, in one form or another. Sometimes these messages are meant to convey important information while other times these messages are meant to sway your colleagues in one direction or another on a decision or a topic. You might need to use persuasion in the workplace to get your employees to do something for you, or for your boss to do something for you or even for your colleagues to help you do something. Either way, having an understanding of how to persuade them can be a very beneficial skill to hone. There are numerous things that you can do to help persuade someone in an argument or to assist you with something.

Persuasion is all about influence. The more influence you have over someone or a group of people, the more power you hold to persuade them. There are many common techniques that help to influence people either on purpose or inadvertently, here are six of the most common (Dean, 2010):

- Likability
- Social proof
- Consistency

- Scarcity
- Authority
- Reciprocity

Likability is just that - the more someone likes you the more influence you hold over them. Influencers can successfully create higher likability by using flattery and highlighting similarities with those they are influencing to create and increase attraction. Social proof is like an avalanche effect - the more followers someone has, the more people follow them. You can hold more influence over someone if you do what you say you are going to do and remain consistent in your words and actions. Scarcity has a lot to do with consumerism and creating a fear of missing out on something, but this can also be applied in the workplace to persuade and influence colleagues. Perhaps if your colleagues view your time as being scarce, they will cherish more.

Authority is a major influencer and is often used to persuade people. People are also influenced by experts. When experts flaunt their knowledge, people become aware and are influenced by those experts. Reciprocity is an influence technique that can be easily misused and abused. When someone owes you something they are more likely to be influenced and persuaded by you. However, you should not go around making people indebted to you for your own personal gain.

The persuasiveness of your argument is not just dependent upon you, it is also dependent upon your audience (Dean, 2019). Your argument or point will be more persuasive if it is personally relevant to your audience. If your audience does not find the message relevant, they are going to stop listening to you and no matter what you say you are not going to be persuasive.

When persuading someone you often need to engage in multiple strong arguments in order to get your message across. Generally speaking, the more strong arguments you have with them the more persuasive you will become. While trying to persuade someone on a topic, it is more beneficial to keep your arguments balanced rather than one-sided. Present a two-sided argument but be sure to shut down the counter-argument to ensure your side of the argument is more appealing.

There are three main goals that you should aim for when trying to persuade someone; affiliation, accuracy and positive self-concept. As humans we are social beings, and as such, we all want to be liked by our peers. Likability and reciprocity are both part of the goal of affiliation. When someone is received as likable and reciprocates, it sends the world a message about their sociability. It is in our nature to join and follow influencers which satisfies the goal of affiliation.

Accuracy is all about doing things right. Those that don't care about how to do things properly don't get very far in life or work. People always want to seek for the right answer, which is where the influencer comes into play. Influencers understand our need to be right and are able to offer their expertise or authority which satisfies our need for accuracy. The goal of accuracy ties into the techniques of social proof and scarcity as experts and influencers are more likely to be right and we don't want to miss out on anything.

The last goal of persuasion is a positive self-concept. People have all sorts of self-protective mechanisms. It takes a very long time for individuals to figure out their place in the world and they don't want to lose that. When we have a certain world view, we do whatever we can to keep that view intact. We want to believe that the things we believe in are, in our eyes, good in some way and help to uphold our self-esteem. This is where influencers can slowly start to persuade you. It starts with a small request and then builds up to larger and larger requests. It can be really amazing the lengths that some will go to maintain that positive view of themselves.

When you are trying to persuade people you should ensure that your message matches your medium. Is what you are trying to persuade people of better received in written or spoken format? Should you speak with them face to face or should you make a video? A very important point is to avoid telling them that you are going to try and persuade them. Doing this will only prime your audience to start preparing their counter arguments when they should be listening to you.

In order to be persuasive, you must first be

familiar with your audience. If they are already somewhat in agreement with you then talking slowly is fine. However, if they are not already in agreement with you, then fast talkers can be more persuasive. Repetition is also beneficial in persuading someone to your point of view. Repeating a statement gives it the illusion of truth which can then lead to the reality of persuasion.

Furthermore, you have to also make sure your audience is ready when you are trying to persuade them. This includes having their attention and minimalizing distractions whenever possible. If your audience is distracted or not paying attention they may not think about your message or argument, which makes it very difficult to persuade someone. It has actually been shown that when people are consuming caffeine, they are more easily persuaded as they are more alert. If you are trying to persuade your audience with a very strong message then it is better to have your audience very focused in on what you are saying. If your message is rather weak, then it is actually better to have your audience slightly distracted. If you are a parent, you have probably experienced this. Your child asks you for something when you are in the middle of something else and, without actually thinking about it, you say yes to their request.

In addition, you have to think very carefully on how you frame your messaging so that it is received in the way you want it to be received. Messages with a positive framing are going to be more persuasive. You must also be a little sneaky and disguise your message so as to not have it come across as persuasive. Your message will be more persuasive if it does not seem to be intended as such.

Confidence also plays a huge role in how your

argument is perceived, both your confidence and your audience's. When you are confident it will help your audience to feel more confident - as such they should be confident in changing their attitude. Confidence also increases when the argument is coming from a credible source. With confidence comes power. The power the audience will feel to change and the power that the influencer holds over the audience.

Lastly, you should avoid trying to persuade strong beliefs or opinions. These are very difficult to change and often people do not budge on them unless they feel an intrinsic need to do so. Never dive into a persuasive argument when there are long standing beliefs and ideas that your audience is committed to. You will only be met with resistance and objection.

How to Effectively Give and Receive Positive Criticism

For most people, being criticized can really hit their ego and self-esteem. However, if done correctly, criticism and critiquing can inspire and uplift individuals and push them to do better in the workplace. Whether or not you are a leader within your organization, you are likely to have to critique a team member or employee at some point. For many people, giving criticism is difficult. However, receiving critique can be even more difficult. Individuals like to feel like they are doing things correctly and that they are accomplished. It doesn't really matter how nicely you put it, it often hurts to hear the truth about your work performance. If you are someone who is consistently striving to improve your work performance, then you might welcome and value the feedback, even if it hurts. If the giver of the feedback is being neutral or coming from a place of positive feedback rather than trying to make the receiver feel bad, that can actually help to build trust through constructive criticism and empathy.

Whether you are giving criticism to a colleague or a subordinate there are certain measures that you can take in order to make sure that your feedback is well received and appreciated. As the receiver of the feedback there are also actions that you can take in order to fully benefit from your feedback. Now, a word of caution, some feedback you receive you might have a warning for, like an employee review. However, some feedback might be unwanted and you will be caught off guard. In either situation, you can take that feedback and make it advantageous to you.

Make sure that you have clear objections. What is the best possible outcome of the critique? If you are the giver of the feedback, do not simply vent without intention; you are not going to achieve anything other than making the other person resent you. If you are the receiver of such criticism and feel that you have come under attack, then do your best to diffuse any tense situation. You can do this by asking the person who is criticizing you what they hope to accomplish with this interaction. In the best case scenario, you will figure out what the root cause of the friction and criticism is, in the worst case scenario, you can make a graceful exit.

When you are going to critique someone or give them feedback of some sort, first consider the environment and the timing. Pick a neutral environment that is free of distractions. There are many situations in the workplace where criticism takes place in front of other employees which can cause embarrassment and shame to the person receiving the criticism. In some work environments a third party is required if an employee is to be "reprimanded," but this can make people feel like they are being ganged up on, so make sure that the third party is neutral and won't cause further friction. Friction can also be minimized by the use of appropriate humor and rapport that has already been built between parties. You can also help to take down defenses of the person you are giving feedback to by sharing your own silly mistakes and personal experiences. This helps for that person to be able to relate to you before addressing their own performance issues.

If you are the person who is being given the feedback and you are feeling threatened or embarrassed, then don't be afraid to speak up about it. Ask the person who is providing you with the feedback to move to a more private area or if you can set up a meeting at another date and time in the near future. Make sure that you are keeping your body language neutral and being open rather than closed off - this will help the person critiquing you to feel more comfortable and relaxed.

Upon critiquing someone it is wise to use fewer words with more meaning behind them. It is likely that the person you are critiquing is going to have a strong internal voice that is causing them anxiety. You are likely to be able to get your point across more if you are short and to the point. The more you try and talk to the person that you are critiquing, the less they are likely to hear. They will become distracted from the key points and it will make it more difficult for them to remember the points you are trying to make. Do your best to plan your conversation in advance and if possible write it down so that the person you are communicating with has something to walk away with and remember the conversation by.

If you are on the receiving end of the criticism, it

is best to let your critics speak their mind and get everything off of their chest. If you try and debate your position you will come off as defensive and closed off. It is better for you to just take the feedback in that moment and agree while revisiting it later for careful consideration. The person that was critiquing you will take you more seriously when your response is contemplated, well thought out and articulated than if you just react to the situation.

You must not approach a critique in a self-serving manner but be able to know your subject well enough to be able to explain how your feedback will benefit them and help them to achieve their desired goals. The person you are giving the feedback to is going to be more open to suggestions if they are invested in the outcome of the critique. If you are able to provide a context for the critique, such as a promotion, then it then becomes vital to their success.

In contrast, if you are the one that is experiencing the critique, then take an objective look at the situation. Step outside of yourself and the situation and objectively look at what is being said. Are you clear on your goals? Is this critique going to help you further your career or is just someone having a bad day rambling on and using you as a target?

Lastly, learn how to use self-critique. Self-critique is two-sided; learning how to do it for yourself and learning how to encourage others to do it. If you are the person giving the feedback, don't just lay out a list of things that they did wrong, give examples of scenarios using an objective viewpoint and ask your subject questions that encourage them to draw their own conclusions. These self-drawn conclusions should focus on the subject's areas of improvement. Ask them questions that help them to take on a manager's perspective of their situation. Use "I" statements or examples from your own experiences that help to take the focus off of them and puts the focus on how you feel.

When it comes to self-critiquing, you should be doing this on a regular basis. Do your best to try and estimate the key points of any feedback before it actually happens. There is a very effective way to disarm your critiques before they start to criticize you and that is to be able to start a conversation about your own failures before someone else is able to. Not only will this disarm your critics but also impress them. This can turn a potential attack into a win-win for both parties.

The Importance of Clear Written Communication Skills in the Workplace

While many employers stress that employees have effective oral and written communication skills, ensuring effective written communication can often be overlooked. When an employee has very effective written communication skills, it can benefit the company in multiple ways, such as ensuring quality communication with customers. Employees with good written communication skills are viewed as intelligent, courteous and detail-oriented.

There is the old adage that you only get one chance to make a first impression, this holds true for written communications as well. The reader of the written communication will form a good impression of the writer if the writing is well-written, organized and free of grammatical errors. Good written communication during the job application process can be crucial to a job offer and increased salary. If an employee has poor writing skills in an external communication, this can reflect poorly on the company overall. If an employee has poor writing skills and their colleagues notice a pattern of poor writing skills, they will likely be viewed as unintelligent (Petersen, 2019).

Excellent written communication skills demonstrate courtesy on the part of the writer. When someone takes the time with their written communications, this shows that they value the reader's time. The reader also benefits from the writer presenting their ideas in a clear and organized manner. If the writer is not able to clearly communicate their message, this takes time and energy from the reader to try and determine what the message is that is trying to be delivered. The reader might even have to ask clarifying questions to try and figure out what the writer is trying to communicate.

Clear communication is vital to sound business decisions both internally and externally. It is much easier for employees to understand projects and to share ideas when objectives are clearly defined and easily understood. For external communications, employees, customers and vendors can more easily understand one another when written communications are clear and free of potential misunderstandings. It is much easier to coordinate goals, meetings and negotiations when written communications are straightforward.

If you are not inherently good at written communications, you can hone your skills here too. There are several ways in which you can work to improve your written communication skills.

Take your time when writing. So often, people make simple and silly mistakes in their writing when they rush. Take your time writing then go back and proofread what you have written. Do not rush through your written communications as quickly as possible but rather as individual mini projects. Always use a grammar checker when writing. Make sure your computer is equipped with a grammar checker or install one.

Don't be afraid to ask for feedback from your colleagues. If you are writing an especially important email, be sure to have your manager or coworker read through the email before sending it on to its recipient. If you feel that you really need some extra help with your writing, take a course on written communications. Most community colleges offer written communications classes and there are also many available online.

The Secret to Being a Proactive Employee at Work

To be proactive means to act before a future event happens; you are causing things to happen rather than just waiting and reacting to things when and as they happen (Scivicque, 2018). Proactive employees are resourceful and are not passive. When employees are proactive they don't need to be micromanaged, they require less detailed instructions from their leadership team and often don't need to be asked to do things and can anticipate the needs of their team. Being proactive can apply to the individual role of the employee or to any extra roles and responsibilities of their team and/or organization. When employees are proactive within their own roles they may find a more effective and productive way of completing their own responsibilities. When an employee is proactive in roles that are outside of their defined job description, this speaks to their organizational citizenship behaviors. An employee with a high organizational citizenship behavior and who is proactive will be more likely to ask their colleagues or manager if they need assistance on a project before being asked to help (Cooley, 2019).

Proactive employees think and act in certain ways that help them to move themselves and their organizations forward.

Employees who are proactive are organized. Their workspace is organized, their schedule is organized and they maintain a positive mindset. When employees are organized and are able to effectively manage their time, they approach tasks in a more effective manner which also allows them to be open to more possibilities in the workplace. A positive mindset in the workplace encourages the employee and their colleagues to look for the best in all situations. Employees who are organized, take stock of situations and remain positive are looked at as ready, willing and able to take on greater responsibilities. They are often viewed as the go-to person and a key problem solver on the team or in the organization. In order to become a more proactive employee, take stock of your current roles and responsibilities within the organization and ask yourself these questions:

- What are your priorities and tasks?
- Which of your priorities can be eliminated, consolidated or shortened?
- What are your regular or less urgent tasks and how can you stay ahead of them?
- When problems arise, how do you solve them?
- How can you plan ahead or anticipate problems before they develop?
- How could you automate tasks to make your work less time consuming and to be more efficient?
- Are there any tasks that you could delegate or that would be better suited for other employees?

Asking yourself these questions and answering them can help you to increase your productivity and become a more proactive employee or leader.

Look around at your coworkers and leaders - is there someone you admire? Someone who always seems to be ahead of the game and everyone seems to go to when an issue arises? If you can, try to spend time with that person and observe their behaviors and gain insight from them. Use what you can learn from them and adapt your own techniques. Some of their techniques might work better for you than others. You need to work to build up your own repertoire and fine-tune the things that work for you and get rid of what doesn't. Let your management or leadership team know that you want to help more or take on greater responsibilities. Don't sit around and wait for someone to ask you to help. You need to be ready and willing to make your own opportunities and show that you want to be more involved and take on more responsibilities.

Goal setting is a very large part of being

proactive. Write down your goals and set deadlines! A goal without a deadline is simply a dream. When you know what you want, it is easier to work towards your outcomes. Small goals can lead to larger goals, so think about working backward. If your goal is to be promoted, then be proactive and figure out how to work backward. This could mean showing your leadership skills by taking on more difficult tasks or working with other employees to help solve problems. Don't get discouraged by setbacks or obstacles that you run into. You have to be willing to step outside of your comfort zone and be resilient when overcoming obstacles. You should be committed to always doing your best work and work on being a role model to others on your team and within your organization. Show that you are passionate about what you are doing and give it your all, even if it's a project that you don't particularly want to work on. Managers and other leaders will take notice.

Being proactive takes a lot of work, so celebrate your successes, no matter how big or small. You have to remain flexible, you can't anticipate every outcome. You need to be able to respond rather than react to unexpected situations; this is a good quality of a proactive employee. While there are certainly situations where it is appropriate to react, proactive employees are flexible and able to manage many different situations.

How to Ask The Right Questions That Get Results

Our brains are wired to ask questions, but in order to get answers that get results, you need to be asking the right questions (Grace, 2018). Asking questions is as much an art as it is a science. If your role in your organization is to get results and keep things moving forward, then you should be well versed in asking questions - quality questions, that is. The quality of the questions that you ask determine the quality of the answers you will receive. Generally speaking, when you start a question with "why," it is unlikely that you will get the answer you are looking for or that any new information will be revealed.

When you start a question with "why," it sounds as though you are placing blame on the person you are speaking with. "Why," questions do not open up dialog and conversation that will lead to getting to the heart of the issue but are often used to confirm a suspicion. When trying to find an answer, asking the right question is half of the battle. Asking "why" questions also puts the person you are asking the question to, in a position that will lead the answer to sound defensive. When you ask "why" questions, you are being lazy as it puts all of the thinking onto the receiver of the question. In order to effectively ask questions, you should frame the question so that it moves the conversation forward rather than trying to hand off the resolution to someone else.

Management teams are trained to give answers, they are not trained to ask good questions. In order to ask better questions, you should observe more beyond a quick glance. Instead of asking why your team didn't finish a project on time, you could ask questions like:

- Which of my team members seem distracted and which seem to be on track?
- Are there any skill sets that the team is missing?
- When does my team seem to produce their best work?
- How do the team dynamics affect the project outcomes?

You see the different areas of concern that are being addressed rather than just placing blame on the team that the project wasn't finished on time. There are many different aspects that could lead to a team not completing the project on time. Perhaps some team members are putting in the work they need to while others are slacking. Or perhaps there are some external factors that are affecting the team's outcomes. Being able to observe your team will help you to ask quality questions that spark further conversation and get to the root cause of issues.

People who are curious tend to be in a better position to be asking the right questions. When professionals like engineers get curious about something, they go deep into the topic. Don't just look for what is obvious or what is on the surface of the issue. Leave all of your judgments and preconceived notions at the door. When you are curious about something, this also opens you up to vulnerability as you can admit that you don't have all of the answers. When it comes to professional and scientific studies, researchers don't hide their mistakes, they publish them in order to help advance their fields. Instead of asking why you (or your team) is failing to find answers you should explore your curiosity. Take a different approach to asking questions curiously. Focus on questions like this:

- What does the solution to this problem look like?
- How would the end-user see this issue and

solution?

Try and look at the problem from all different angles and come up with various perspectives. Ask other people their perspective on the issue or check to see what others have done in similar situations, which leads me to my next point, recognizing patterns.

When you are able to recognize patterns in problems you can then arrive at a solution quicker. When you are able to get the pattern right you can then scale your design as it should consistently work. Instead of focusing on why you have not yet found a solution, focus on what has already worked and how you can consider the problem from a different perspective.

Quality questions also show empathy. Genuine and quality questions are not leading in nature nor do they ask for anything in return. The questions you are asking should not be about trying to find the quickest or easiest solution but rather finding a long-term solution. Get to the root of the problem and stop asking why the problem exists but rather how you can get closer to the source of the issue. Here are some empathetic questions to consider:

- How can your team get closer to the source of the issue?
- What can each individual do to help realize the issue at hand?
- What can you do to make the solution more practical and easier to understand?

Finally, you must be present and engaged when asking questions. Being present is about understanding the culture surrounding the issue and being able to change the lens in which you view the problem. Changing the lens can mean looking to different environments and industries to observe how others might be resolving issues. Instead of asking why a product or service is not selling you need to look beyond the product or service itself and look to the consumers. Ask instead:

- Are the buyers experiencing resistance of some kind?
- What can you do to remove barriers to the customers?

Asking truly effective questions stems from incorporating all five of the aforementioned areas. You must be able to observe, bring curiosity to the problem, be able to recognize patterns surrounding the issue, empathize with the end user and be present in cultural differences. Quality question asking provides a sense of ownership that promotes leveraged thinking by revealing concepts. You can start to ask better questions by utilizing creative thinking, openness and inclusivity.

How to Professionally Report to Your Leadership Team on a Project Status

Developing a professional report on a project that you are working on can go a long way to showcasing your communication skills to your leadership team. Being able to professionally report on the status of a project is not something that many people are skilled at; even the best project managers can struggle with this. It simply comes down to a lack of understanding from the perspective of the project manager (Redmond, 2018). Your manager is most likely being pressed for information from their manager on the status of the project and it has now ended up in your lap on the reporting of the project status. There are a few basic rules that you can adhere to, to build your reputation as someone who knows how to effectively report on the status of a large and important project. You will be able to keep your management team informed and keep the project successfully moving forward.

First and foremost, you need to take on the perspective of your manager or management team which you will be reporting to. If you are the one in charge of reporting the status of an important project then it shouldn't come as a surprise that your manager is going to consume any important information on the project that they can get. If you are able to build an excellent report on the status of the project, your manager doesn't have to worry about getting involved and can remain informed about the health and direction of the project. Your boss needs to regularly obtain information about the project in order to share with their boss. When you are on top of things, your boss will also look like they are on top of things which can be a benefit to you.

Even if you are working on a project that is less important, you should take the reporting of that project just as seriously. It is beneficial to your manager to be able to look at a short report for a project that they can easily skim over the details of to ensure that everything is on track. Your job in being able to professionally report a project comes down to being able to distil all of the information into easily digestible chunks that are simple to understand while presenting the most basic and essential elements of the project. There are three main components to writing an excellent project status report. You must include the three main components (overall, milestones and issues), how to organize the status of your report, what brief details to include, the key data to include, any issue management and the expected results.

The three main components that you should be including in your project report that will have your manager jumping for joy over your stellar project reporting skills are the overall, milestones and issues. The overall of the project is the general overall health of the project. The management team should be able to detect if the project is in trouble. As the one reporting on the project, you might not be aware of all the issues of the project and your manager should be able to quickly determine if the project is in trouble from what you are reporting. The next important component is the project milestones. The milestones are major accomplishments that have been completed at specific dates. Managers should be able to see which milestones have been completed, which ones are on track and which might be behind. This allows the management team to see an overall view of the schedule of the project and help them to adjust accordingly if necessary. Lastly, the third major component of the project that you should report on, is any issues that have arisen. If there have been any obstacles for the successful completion of the project, you should be sure to include these in your report. This helps the management team determine if they need to make adjustments or step in and offer further assistance.

Up next is being able to effectively organize your project report. You should be starting at the highest level and working your way down to the lower level stuff. Make sure to put the overall project health first; this way, a manager can immediately tell if something needs to be done with the project. If the manager is concerned about the overall project health they can look at further details within the project health, look at scheduled dates and the issues that could be affecting the project deadlines. If you are really good at reporting, you should be able to report the issues that are causing the most issues by priority.

In addition, your project report should include the brief details. They need to be clear, concise and crisp in order for the management team to quickly consume them with little effort. Considering your manager likely has many projects that they are managing, they have very little time to sit down and read your project report, so make sure you are only including the details that they absolutely need to know. You don't need to narrate your project report but rather be as to the point as possible. For example, rather than writing in paragraphs, use short, bulleted points. Reduce the information as much as possible without cutting out any vital information. Avoid adding any adverbs and adjectives or any unnecessary labeling. For example, do not put "date: 1/2/2019" but rather just the date as "1/2/2019" already signifies a date and does not need explanation.

You must ensure that all key data is included in

your project report. This will let your management team know the overall health of the project, the project milestones and any issues that are present. The key data points that you should be including in your project report are:

- The name of the project.
- Any project identification numbers or other identifiers.
- The overall health of the project.
- The percentage you expect to be completed at certain milestones.
- The percentage that are actually completed at certain milestones.
- The number of days you are ahead or behind on the project.
- The number of issues that you are facing preventing the project from moving forward.
- The number of any "normal" issues the project is experiencing.

These elements of data should provide a sound enough overview of the project that your leadership can take a quick look over. Your leadership team needs to see more than just the overall health of the project, they need to be able to see a very quick overview of the timeline, milestones and issues to determine if they should get involved and assist the project. When giving an overview on project milestones you should include the milestone name, the percentage of completion of the milestone, the planned start and finish date and the actual start and finish date. There are many different ways to present the milestones using colors and fancy charts. Don't go for what looks best, go for what is the most practical and easy to understand. You want to create clarity, not more confusion.

When it comes to communicating project issues, you should present these at the end of your project report. This section should include all the various things your leadership team needs to know about the issues the project is experiencing. This can include the ticket number if you have some kind of project issue ticketing system, the name of the issue, the date and time the issue was reported, the priority or severity of the issue, the name of the person who is currently handling the issue, the estimated time the issue is going to be resolved and the current activity of the issue.

Once you have become great at communicating with your leadership team on the status of projects, one of two things will generally happen. Either your leadership team will talk to you less because they feel that you have everything under control, or they will converse with you more to try and stay on top of any issues and get more details out of you. They are less likely going to be constantly asking you about the status of the project as you will already have provided it to them. If your management team is still asking you for status reports, you are either not sending them enough, not sending them to the right people or not sending a good enough status report. Your leadership team should not have to continuously ask you for status reports but rather be able to passively consume them. Employees that are able to produce quality project reports are few and far between. An employee that can present a project in a clear and concise manner is much more beneficial to the company than someone who can make fancy charts and graphs.

Chapter Summary

Developing effective communication skills at work is something that anyone is capable of. With your communication toolbox stocked full, you can persuade management, get your employees on board and ensure that your message is always being effectively communicated.

There are many ways to communicate both verbally and non-verbally. Considering that 90% of your overall communication is non-verbal, it is very important that you are well aware of your body language and other non-verbal cues while at work. One of the quickest things that you can do to improve your communication through body language is to maintain eye contact while speaking with someone. Here are a few other tips and tricks for effectively using your body language.

- Keep an erect posture.
- While sitting, lean in towards someone when speaking or listening to them.
- Be aware of how others are using their body language.
- Don't fidget.
- Be aware of cultural and gender differences.
- Keep an open and relaxed stance.
- Be conscious of your facial expressions.

With each message we send, there are both verbal and non-verbal cues. You should be practicing various forms of body language and ensuring that you are not coming off to other people as smug, arrogant or lacking confidence.

Being a better listener at work is all part of effective communication. Sometimes there might be a lot of environmental noise that you have to work through. However, if you take these tips into consideration, you should be able to effectively communicate in any work environment.

- Be quiet and let others speak without trying to come up with what you are going to say next.
- Repeat back to the person you are speaking with what you said in your own words.
- Maintain eye contact when the person is speaking, this will help you to retain information.
- Remember what someone is trying to say to you as if you will have to recall it later on.
- Minimize distractions from technology.
- Ask open-ended questions to clarify what was said.
- Be mentally and physically prepared to listen.
- Be present in the moment and listen.
- If you are unable to effectively hold a conversation with someone, schedule an

appropriate time in the future.
- Ensure that your verbal and non-verbal communication are cohesive.

Workplaces are becoming more and more diverse. It is vital to understand the importance of inclusivity in the workplace. It is a well-established fact that men and women communicate differently and gender stereotypes are inadvertently perpetuated by our everyday conversations. Effective communicators are able to hear facts and ideas and listen for the values and feelings behind them. Male leaders would benefit from specifically asking for input from their female counterparts.

Persuasive communication is also a very effective skill to have, particularly in the workplace. Knowing how to get people "on your side" so to speak, can help to influence people. People can be persuaded through likability, social proof, consistency, scarcity, authority and reciprocity.

The more of one of these that you have, the more influence you hold over people. The effectiveness of your influence is not just about you, it is also dependent on your audience. Your audience needs to find your message relevant in order to be persuaded.

There are three main goals you should focus on when trying to persuade someone; affiliation, accuracy and positive self-concept. If you have some work to do to persuade people, then talking faster and repeating what you are saying will help people to believe in what you are saying. You also need to be sure that your audience is paying attention to what you are saying. When persuading people, you also need to be confident in your delivery.

When giving feedback, ensure that you are using

"I" statements and framing the critique in a positive manner. It is also important to be able to self-critique and disarm your critics before they are able to start pointing fingers at what you have done wrong.

Employees who are proactive are able to anticipate the needs of their team while being resourceful. Proactive employees are also not afraid to ask for help from their leadership team.

Coming up in the next chapter, you will learn how to effectively handle difficult situations and people in the workplace.

Chapter Three: How to Effectively Handle Difficult Situations and People in the Workplace

It happens in every workplace; there is at least one person that you work with who always seems to make things more difficult. At some point in your work career, you are going to work with difficult people or have to deal with difficult situations. It can be either internally or externally that you will experience difficult situations or people. However, that does not mean that it has to cause you a lot of stress or derail any of your goals.

How To Deal With Difficult People In Your Workplace; Coworkers or Customers

If you have ever worked in customer service, it is highly likely that you have had to deal with a difficult customer. In every workplace, there are going to be difficult people that you will have to work with. This might be clients, customers, vendors, colleagues or your leadership team (we will cover that next). Learning to deal with difficult people is a skill that is well worth spending time honing. While learning this skill can certainly be challenging, it can also prove to be very rewarding.

When you learn to deal with difficult people in your work environment, you can drastically improve employee morale and your satisfaction in the workplace (Heathfield, 2019). When you are able to address issues with a difficult coworker, it helps to create an overall better work environment. Difficult people in the work environment come in a wide variety but how you deal with them depends on you. It depends on your self-esteem, your self-confidence, your professional courage, as well as how often you have to work with that person.

It is generally easier to deal with a difficult person if other people in the workplace also find them difficult to work with. If that coworker is generally obnoxious or disliked, you can recruit other colleagues to help you address the situation. It might be wise to get your leadership team involved to help diffuse tense situations or when having to deal with difficult people. If you wait too long, things might spiral out of control and end up in a very negative situation. This could lead to the difficult person even undermining your professional credibility, attacking you and making you look bad.

You might even encounter situations at your work where you feel bullied. This can be outright and obvious or it can be much more subtle. You might work with a bully if you regularly feel intimidated or dread even going near that employee. Bullies tend to yell at other employees, insult them, put people down, physically or psychologically abuse or threaten people. Being bullied at work is not uncommon, it actually happens quite often. A bully might talk over you in meetings, regularly criticize your work or steal credit for your ideas or work performance.

Difficult people at work can also include those that are always negative. Some people, it doesn't matter what you do, they can just never seem to be positive. They always seem to be complaining about things, they don't like the company, they don't like their job and are just generally unpleasant to be around. Even while you practice positivity, it can be difficult to be around these people because they always seem to drag everyone down. Your best bet to deal with this kind of difficult person is to just avoid them altogether. If you can't avoid them and have to work with them at some point, then just do your best to remain positive.

There are many different types of difficult people that you can find in your workplace. Some of them just have a generally difficult personality while others seem to target you and your efforts. It doesn't really matter what kind of difficult person you are dealing with, it is not going to benefit you by simply avoiding them. You need to face the situation and handle it head-on. Most often, difficult people and situations become worse if left unaddressed.

You don't want to leave the issue of dealing with a difficult person unaddressed as it is only going to cause you anxiety and leave you miserable. You should not let others affect your attitude at work. If you are being treated in an unprofessional manner, do your best to understand why this is happening to you. You don't want to let your feelings fester and lead you to become irrational and thus react to this person in an unprofessional manner.

If you can avoid the person causing your stress at work, then do so. However, this is not always possible. If you complain about them to other coworkers this can quickly make you look like the bad guy (or girl) and you will be labeled as a whiner. Even if you have a manager or leadership team that is very understanding, they may begin to wonder why it is that you cannot solve your issues with said coworker yourself. If others feel that you are not able to handle difficult individuals at work then you too could quickly be labeled as a difficult person to work with. Not only is this a very troublesome title to get rid of, it can wreak havoc on your career.

In the event that there is someone you find difficult to work with, there are a few steps that you can take in order to clarify that is indeed the situation. Take some time to really consider if that person is actually the problem and it is not actually you. That is harsh to say, I know, but sometimes you are the problem and you don't even realize it. Talk with another trusted colleague to gauge their reaction to the person. See if you can approach the person you are having an issue with and see if you can speak with them about your issues. They might be doing something that they don't even realize they are doing. After you have spoken with them, has their behavior changed in any way? Has it gotten better or worse? Have they begun to single you out or do you find working with them enjoyable now?

You can also use humor to try and diffuse a tense situation. This is not effective for everyone. Some people are not naturally humorous and trying to be funny just might sound like making fun of the person. If being funny and joking does not come naturally to you, then don't do it.

On the chance that you have tried to deal with the difficult person on your own without success, it might be time to involve your leadership team. Don't address the issue as a personal problem that you have with that person, but rather an issue with productivity. Make sure to be specific and provide examples of how they are affecting your productivity. If you have separate managers, it is wise to include both party's bosses.

In the event that there are other individuals at work that are having issues with said employee, try to rally them together. This does not mean ganging up on them. This means taking the issues that you are all having with the person to your boss or to their boss. This might help to convince the leadership team that there really is an issue and it is not just one person picking on another.

How to Deal With a Difficult Boss at Work

Dealing with difficult bosses at work can be a whole other challenge. You can't take your issues to your boss because they are the one you are having issues with. It is bound to happen at some point that you will have to deal with a difficult boss in your work career. While it would be great if every boss that you have is trustworthy, competent, kind and fair, that is not likely the reality. A difficult boss can drastically affect employee engagement, productivity and the desire of employees to contribute to the team. Generally speaking, when an employee makes the decision to quit their job it is often due to their boss, not necessarily the company or the job itself. Having a boss that you can get along with is critical to employee satisfaction and retention.

It is unfortunate but sometimes when people are in a position of power they abuse that power and can become bullies to their employees. They may take credit for an employee's work, control them and never provide them with positive feedback. Just as with less than desirable coworkers, your boss might not realize that he is bad (Heathfield, 2018).

The undesirable qualities in your boss might come from a lack of training or micromanaging. Your boss might feel overwhelmed and not know how to give you the proper direction or support. If your boss was promoted too quickly, they might not realize their full responsibilities. Bosses from a different generation and different cultural backgrounds can also have conflicting views and cause friction in the workplace.

Try and resolve any issues you are having with your boss by speaking with them first. Let them know what you need as far as direction, support and feedback are concerned. If you have access to another manager, seek out a mentor to help you figure out how to deal with your boss. Have a heart-to-heart with your manager and ask them how you can help them reach their goals. This can help them to realize that you want to help them and are willing to go the extra mile.

On the chance that speaking to your boss doesn't work, then you might need to go above his or her head and go to their boss or to human resources to resolve any issues. If you do go to your boss's boss or to human resources you might not fully ever find out what they did to resolve the issues, but you should at least give it some time to take effect. If there are other coworkers who have experienced your boss's unfair or rude behaviors, work with them collectively and visit human resources or their manager to discuss the situation.

What you need to realize from the start is that you have the right to work in a safe and professional environment. Don't get into any kind of public screaming match but try to draw his/her attention to his/her behavior privately when you have the opportunity. If you have made attempts to change without any success, then see if you are able to transfer departments.

How to Tactfully Handle Noisy and Disruptive Coworkers

You can't always choose your work environments or who is present in your work environment. You might unwillingly get stuck sitting by someone who is often loud and disruptive. Disruptive coworkers can not only wreak havoc on your productivity but also cause undue stress and tension in the workplace (Zenbooth, 2019). If you are dealing with a disruptive coworker, there are several things that you can do in order to tactfully handle any noisy and disruptive coworkers.

Try and handle the problem from your end. You might not realize it but some people are more sensitive to noise than others and if you are one of those people, someone that talks at a regular volume to others might feel overwhelming to you. If you are able to, bring a pair of noise-canceling headphones and listen to soothing music while you are by your noisy coworker. Just remember that you have headphones on before you start talking to someone else, you don't want to end up being the noisy coworker.

It is also in your interest to just be polite and ask if your coworkers are able to keep it down and explain why. Perhaps you need to take an important phone call or the like; it is a great excuse to communicate with your coworkers that work does not need to be loud. If you generally have a sense of humor, try making a cute or funny sign to cue to your colleagues to keep it down. However, this is only really a short-term solution if your coworkers are loud or noisy all of the time.

Generally speaking, if you are a rather polite person you can get away with simply asking others to keep quiet. Let them know that you really enjoy the fun work culture, but you just feel a little overwhelmed or distracted by how loud it can get at times. Hopefully, your colleagues are understanding and will work to keep the area around your workstation a little quieter. Unless your coworkers are just mean people or they don't like you for some reason, they should politely abide. You can also do your best to make it a two-way conversation and ask them if there is anything that you do that is disruptive to their work. This shows that you are also taking their productivity and workplace satisfaction into consideration.

You also have to be sure that you are not reinforcing the talkative or noisy behavior of your coworkers. If you have a coworker that is particularly talkative and they are consistently trying to talk with you, do your best to politely avoid them. When someone is being very talkative this is often attention-seeking behavior. If your chatty coworker continues to try and speak with you, respond to any questions they have with a short and to-the-point answer, then go back to what you were doing and divert your eye contact. This is a way to use your body language to let them know that the conversation is over. If they keep on trying to talk to you, just let them know that you have a lot of work to get finished and you are not trying to be rude but you need to focus on your task at hand.

Also make sure that you are setting a good example for your coworkers. If you are approached by a rather loud colleague, move the conversation somewhere where you will not disrupt other coworkers. If they don't want to move the conversation somewhere where they will not be disrupting others, simply ask them to lower their voice so as not to disturb those that are working. This should hopefully set an example for your loud coworkers.

If you are having difficulty with getting your coworkers to quiet down when you have to take an important call or need to get your work done, then scope out a quiet location. Most office buildings have spare conference rooms or empty offices that you can use either on a regular basis or on occasion for taking those important phone calls.

While going to your supervisor or human resources might be a last option, it might be your only option. Sometimes no matter how polite you are with your coworkers, there are some times where they just might not care about your work and would rather annoy you with their loud antics. It should always be the goal of human resources to provide everyone with a harmonious working environment. Human resources should be able to tactfully handle the situation and address it in a general manner rather than singling anyone out as being the loud one or the person making the complaint.

How to Manage Difficult Situations at Work and Keep Your Cool

It is one thing to deal with difficult people and bosses at work, it is another to deal with difficult situations. Difficult situations can arise with customers, with other coworkers, with vendors or your boss. Difficult situations at work, just as with difficult people, cause stress and anxiety. Difficult work situations are caused by a lack of control. It might feel that everyone is out to get you and that there is nothing you can do about it. However, there are things that you can do about it!

Even if you are generally a level-headed person, your work environment can get the best of you. Bottling up all of your frustrations from work is not going to benefit anyone. It is likely that you will end up taking out your anger and frustrations on unwitting family members, like your kids or spouse. While we all know that exercise has many benefits, one more benefit is to be able to better handle difficult work situations. If you are able to squeeze in a brisk walk or quick run before headed out to work, this can not only provide you with mental clarity but also give you some energy for the day. You can easily release all the tension you are holding onto from work by working out for about 30 minutes per day. It might require you getting up a little bit earlier but I can promise you the benefits far outweigh the inconvenience of getting up a little earlier. When you have energy for the day and your mind is clear, you are able to focus better and not act irrationally to situations and be able to calmly deal with difficult work situations and coworkers.

It might also be beneficial to get an outside opinion of the situation. Overthinking situations can trap your mind in a continual downward spiral. It might feel like sometimes you can't escape your work life and that your entire life revolves around your work. It can become very overwhelming when the only point of view of the situation is your own. If you are finding your workplace difficult to deal with, then get out! Now, I am not saying that you should quit, what I am saying is that you should find a way to get out of work and to get your head out of work. Meet a friend who is not your coworker out for lunch or go for a walk. A friend that you do not work with might be able to offer an outside perspective on the situation. You can tell them exactly how you feel without having to worry about any backlash from your employer or coworkers.

Just as with overthinking things, it is possible to overanalyze your situation too. Much of the stress and anxiety about your work situation might stem from the feeling of just not being able to get out of the difficult situation. Your mind can be very powerful, in either a positive or negative light. It is easy to get caught up in the pattern of overthinking and trying to figure out everything that is going on at work, like who your boss is currently favoring or why you always seem to end up in difficult situations there. What you might not realize is that most of the situations are due to overthinking and are in your head. Most often these difficult working situations are not the actual reality but rather your mind running wild. Turn those negative thoughts about your work into actions. Focus on your work. Find a task within a project and throw yourself into it. Focus on making contributions to your workplace and gain back control over the situations you deal with at work (Miglani et al., 2019).

How to Overcome Your Coworkers' Poor Communication Skills

Even if you have become a first-class communicator in your workplace, it is unlikely that all of your coworkers will follow suit. While being able to communicate something to your team should seem like a simple process, there are any things that can interfere with getting the message across clearly.

There are certain ways to tell if you are working with a poor communicator. If the person you are speaking with doesn't seem to be communicating back to you or isn't giving you any feedback, it is likely that they are not great at communicating. This can also happen if you have a colleague who isn't getting any feedback either. They just might be talking too much and you should know by now that when it comes to effective communication you should be listening twice as much as you are talking.

You might also find that your coworker lacks effective communication skills if they use "you" directives rather than "I" statements. For example, *"you never finish your part of the project on time."* An example of using an "I" statement would be something like; *"I feel like I am taking on more responsibility for the project."* Using "you" statements can make those people they are speaking with that they are being talked at rather than talked to. It might also feel that blame is being placed on them rather than having a neutral overtone. Do your coworkers react to ideas that are presented to them by shooting them down or do they engage in discussion about the idea? If they automatically shut down the idea then they are not very good communicators.

Poor communicators also don't really ever address the problem but rather the people. In addition to shooting down an idea they might also put down the people who presented the idea. An employee is never going to get positive results by spewing out negative comments to other coworkers. Individuals who are poor communicators also disregard or invalidate the feelings of their coworkers. They might also use passive-aggressive talk or sarcasm as a way of responding to professional and personal interactions.

You can work to overcome poor communicators by encouraging them to use effective communication skills. Don't play the blame game with them though, just provide them with a good example of effective communication and gently point out the things they could improve on.

How to Keep People from Wasting Your Time at Work

No matter who you are, time is your most precious commodity. In a work setting there are plenty of ways that people can waste your time, e.g. not showing up for a meeting (and not having the courtesy to cancel in advance) (Galek, 2019), stalling your work with their inability or disrupting your work in other ways. People can also waste your time by being time suckers. This can happen if you are an especially nice person who wants to help people; you can easily get taken advantage of. As a colleague and especially if you are a leader, there is a delicate balance between helping others and having your time wasted.

Time is precious; no one has unlimited time to be helping others, they generally have their own work to get done. You might think you are being helpful and responsive to your colleagues and their needs which of course is going to benefit the company, right? This is not always the case. You can't always say yes to every person every time. When your time is being taken up by someone or something else, you are not able to give your time to other more important people or tasks. If you have the same colleagues always coming to you for help on certain things, they can then learn to become dependent on you rather than trying to figure it out for themselves, which can become a vicious cycle. These colleagues are also wasting their own time by having to reach out to you all of the time and not being able to figure it out on their own. Perhaps instead of figuring out something on their own, they put it off until you can help them (Stachowiak, 2019). This can waste their time, yours and the company's.

While you want to be able to help your colleagues, there have to be rules and boundaries set in place to prevent people from wasting your time and to keep projects moving forward. Whether or not if you are a leader in your organization, it is not to say that you should always shut others out to avoid time wasters. You have to be smart about your time and how you spend it so that you aren't "busy" all day without actually getting anything done. Here are a few strategies to help you get more done during the day and ensure that you are also not feeling like you are blowing off your coworkers:

1) Try and book appointments with your coworkers (Stachowiak, 2019). This can work in two different ways. If you need to have a longer discussion with someone or if they need to have a longer discussion with you. If you are approached by a coworker and it is clear that their discussion with you is going to take more than five minutes, then you can book an appointment with them to fully discuss the issue at hand. I'm sure you have dealt with people like this before; they say it's only going to take a few minutes, but in reality, it takes much longer. Setting an appointment will not only benefit you but also will benefit them. When you have time to have a discussion you are able to be present for it rather than thinking about when this person is going to stop talking. Making an appointment with someone to discuss an issue

allows both parties to get all of their questions answered fully and be able to focus on the most important factors of the discussion.

2) If someone seems to keep coming to you for little things here and there throughout the day, have them make a list. When they think of something they need to discuss with you, have them write it down either on a piece of paper or in a shared document. If the discussion is not urgent then you should be able to access their list and set an appointment to have a discussion about things with them. This works well because you can send them a meeting agenda in advance to make sure they will have all of their questions answered.

3) When you do set a meeting or appointment with someone, make sure you are setting a time limit and sticking to it! While setting a meeting can help to avoid wasting time, this can also

backfire on you. If you set a meeting for 30 minutes, and 90 minutes later you are still discussing topics, this defeats the purpose of having a meeting set in the first place. If you are part way through the meeting and you realize that it is going to take a lot longer to resolve the issues at hand, then set up another time to talk. A tactic that you can use to make sure that your meetings don't run over is to book another appointment right after so that you are obligated to end the meeting on time.

4) Make sure you are asking questions to help your colleagues to try and solve their own problems. While it can feel great when others come to you for answers, people need to figure out how to solve their own problems. Just giving people the answers all of the time is not going to help them in the long run and is only going to make them dependent on you. Don't just do other people's work for them. Even if you are not

technically a leader within your organization, you can still act like a leader and possess leadership qualities. You can provide coaching or mentoring to colleagues, but don't just do their work and give them all the answers.

5) When it comes to not giving people all the answers, you also have to be sure that you are helping them to come up with solutions as well. Sometimes people just need to vent, and that is ok. However, the conversation you are having should be focused on finding solutions rather than simply complaining or venting. If you and your colleague are unable to come up with a solution, ask them to schedule another appointment with you when they have found a solution to the problem. This can be difficult at first, but this signals to your coworkers that you are serious about your time and are not going to wait around for them to come and complain to you.

Chapter Summary

Regardless of the workplace, you are bound to run into difficult people and or situations. Whether you are dealing with clients, customers or vendors, there are bound to be difficult situations that arise and difficult people that you have to work with. When you are able to handle difficult people in a tactful manner, you will improve your overall morale and workplace satisfaction. When you regularly practice positivity at work, you cancel out others' negativity and are able to defend yourself from their negative ways. While it is ideal that you avoid difficult people altogether, this might not always be an option. In the worst-case scenario, you will have to recruit your management team or human resources to help resolve a difficult issue or to deal with a difficult person.

In the unfortunate circumstance that you get stuck with a very difficult boss, you can always take the route of "killing them with kindness". However, having a difficult boss can make a work situation very distressing as you might have to go above their heads to their boss or human resources. So often people quit a job they love or a company that they enjoy working for just because the person they report directly to is very difficult to work with. Unfortunately, people in positions of power can abuse that position, causing distress and frustration among their team.

You might also run into the problem of having to deal with noisy and disruptive coworkers, especially if you do not have your own office. It is best to handle these people and situations with rapport and humor when possible. Ensure that you are setting a good example for your coworkers and scoping out quieter locations if necessary.

Dealing with difficult situations at work can lead to high levels of stress and anxiety. Anxiety-ridden work environments can get the best of even the most level-headed individuals. Do your best to stay focused on your work and making positive contributions to your organization.

If you have been really practicing your effective communication skills, it is likely that you will begin to realize how ineffective other people's communication skills are. You can encourage your colleagues to brush up on their communication skills by using "I" statements, giving positive feedback and addressing the problem rather than the person or people involved in the problem.

Another very large issue that can often arise at work is other people wasting your time. If you have a colleague who is constantly asking you for a few minutes of your time that then turns into

45 to 60 minutes, ask them to schedule a meeting with you so that you may discuss all of their concerns. You can also have your colleague make a list of things that they would like to discuss with you in order to speed up your interaction and address all of their concerns. Don't forget to stick to your meeting times and don't let your coworkers bully you into wasting your time to fill their needs.

In the next chapter, you will learn tips and tricks on how to be the most effective leader you can be.

Chapter Four: How to Be The Most Effective Leader You Can Be

What does being an effective leader mean to you? Businesses are built on successful leadership. Leaders need to be flexible and able to easily adapt to situations (Daskal, 2019). Leaders also need to be able to delegate tasks effectively. An effective leader also needs to be charismatic as well as an effective communicator. Leaders should be able to set goals effectively and help to move their teams forward by inspiring and leading with a shared vision. And of course, be able to take action!

How to Become a More Charismatic Leader

When you think of someone who is charismatic, who comes to mind? Winston Churchill, Richard

Branson?

Often times people think that being charismatic is something that someone is born with. However, you can learn to be charismatic with a little practice. Leaders that are charismatic are influential, persuasive and inspire others. People are drawn to charismatic people; they want to be part of their circle of influence, they want to learn from you (Giang, 2019). Charismatic leaders don't require a long list of qualifications or education to qualify them as credible.

Someone who is charismatic knows how to make others feel that they are intelligent, impressive and fascinating (Giang, 2012). People who are charismatic have a way of uplifting others and making them feel good about themselves. Charismatic leaders are present with their audience. You can pause before answering or asking questions of those you are speaking with. Don't just be waiting for someone to finish what they are saying before you start talking and thinking about your rebuttal in the meantime. Make sure your face is showing some type of interest and you aren't sitting there with a blank stare on your face - this is not going to win you any fans.

There are several things that you can do if you would like to become a more charismatic leader. First, you have to build a connection with your audience. Some leaders choose to lead just by using their authority; this leaves your colleagues and those employees that report to you feeling like you are the boss and they have to remain under your command. Charismatic leaders are able to connect with people on various levels, sometimes even on a personal level. Talk to people and get to know them. People love to talk about themselves or their kids. It is also beneficial to ask for your colleagues' input. Don't just spew off your demands and expect people to follow along. Ask them their opinions and if they feel things are headed in the right direction. Doing this on an occasional basis will let your team members know that their leader is there to do more than just lead them, their leader is there to listen to them and learn from them.

Charismatic leaders put people at ease and don't make their audience or colleagues feel too serious. Charismatic leaders squash tension with light humor while still ensuring that their team remains productive. While it is a delicate balance, a good and charismatic leader is able to maintain a balance between being too serious and being too easygoing. As a charismatic leader, you are able to share stories that show your vulnerability and that you are indeed human. Leaders who possess a lot of confidence and are very likable are often seen as charismatic. Charisma is also a quality that people who are able to sway individuals with their arguments to their point of view possess. With great confidence also comes great humility and a charismatic leader will understand that they are not the smartest person in the room. This helps to bring confidence to the team and to the individuals on the team by empowering them.

Trustworthiness and not going back on their promises is also another trait of charismatic leaders. There is nothing worse than a leader who says they are going to do one thing and ends up doing something else and breaking the trust of their team. Charismatic leaders also have a very strong commitment to their goals and lead by example. They don't mind being in the trenches with their team and are in it to get the job done! They are also able to motivate their team to get done what they need to get done.

The Essentials to Becoming a Master Communicator

With any business, learning to become a master communicator is key. Just as with any skill, you can learn to communicate effectively with a few simple tactics. First of all, you need to discover your own individual voice. Everyone has a different personality and how you interact and speak with people will set you apart from others. Other people will recognize you from your voice, your tone and how you verbally carry yourself (Adams, 2019). Stand out without being arrogant or obnoxious.

Mastering communication also requires confidence. Confidence portrays that you understand what you are talking about and are able to communicate your message to others. Even if you are generally introverted, you can still speak with confidence. People you are speaking with are able to tell if you are confident in what you are saying or if you are just trying to avoid looking like a fool. No matter the situation you find yourself in, you should remain confident.

When you are communicating with others, you should not worry about speaking fast but rather slow down a bit. Those that you are communicating with need to be able to understand what you are saying. Speaking fast is not necessary in most cases and can actually lead to miscommunication. Your communications should also have a purpose (Adams, 2019). You should be able to share your message with others in an effective manner by portraying a clear focus.

Master communicators are also able to engage with their audience. Being a master communicator isn't always about the person who is speaking, it is also about the people or person they are speaking to. Engaging with people, saying their names, making eye contact, shaking hands and so on lets them know that you care about your message and how they are receiving the message.

How Leaders Effectively Set Goals

Whether you are an employee who is striving to be a leader or you are already leading a team, setting goals within your organization is important. Goal setting as a leader can be even more important as you are not only setting goals for yourself but also for those on your team. Just as with many other goals in life, you should set

S.M.A.R.T. goals and make them simple, measurable, achievable, realistic, and time bound. These goals are ones that you can set by yourself or with your team. You should focus on no more than five for the next 12 months and they should be very clear (Peck, 2017).

Goal setting is important to leaders for several reasons. Goal setting shows that you as the leader are competent in achieving performance results. Setting and achieving goals with your team instills confidence in you and themselves. When you see that they can set and achieve targeted results they will want to keep going with achieving more goals.

When you set goals for your team, it helps to give each person direction. Each individual involved should understand their part in the goal and target their efforts to achieve the goal. When you, as a leader, set goals and your team works to achieve them, this is also letting you assess their abilities at the same time. Goal setting and achieving also shows ownership of goals and projects.

S.M.A.R.T. goals are always the safest way to set goals either by yourself or when working with a team. Remember that your S.M.A.R.T. goals should be specific, measurable, achievable, results-oriented, and timebound. You cannot say, "let's get more clients!" and use that as a goal. A S.M.A.R.T. goal for getting more clients would be something like: "Make X# of outbound sales calls per day, follow up with X# of current clients and work to obtain X# of sales per week/day." While not all of your goals will be completely in your hands and might depend on outside factors (like clients), having a S.M.A.R.T. goal helps to make those goals specific and easy for everyone to understand.

In addition to focusing on S.M.A.R.T. goals, you also have to realize that there are two different types of goals, performance and learning. Performance goals focus on specific end goals and results, such as getting more clients or building a new prototype. Learning goals focus on creativity and expending on skill development, such as increasing your emotional intelligence or other soft skills. Whenever possible, get the people on your team to help with goal setting. Generally speaking, when someone helps to build their goal they are going to be more committed to it.

How to Clarify Your Values at Work

Your values are things that you should adhere to both inside and outside of work. They are beliefs and ideas that you have identified as core principles and are an integral part of who you are. Your values can be things like honesty, humility, self-respect, respecting others or success (however you may define that). Before you ever choose your career and/or accept a job, you should have your values defined. Don't worry, it's not too late to start defining your values.

There are two different types of values, intrinsic and extrinsic (Rosenberg McKay, 2018). The intrinsic values, when it comes to establishing values at work, are those that have to do with the actual work tasks performed. Examples of intrinsic values result in job satisfaction and engagement. The extrinsic values are the results of the by-products of your job. This has to deal with what you get out of your work, not what you put into it. Extrinsic values include things like your salary, job security and recognition.

While it is good practice to identify your work values very early on in your work career, it is not too late to identify them now. There is a simple inventory that you can do to access your work values in which you define them and number them from one to ten. This is called a work values inventory (Rosenberg McKay, 2018). Write down ten of your values and number them from one to ten with one being the most important and ten being the least important. While you can recruit a professional to do a work values inventory with you, you can also complete one easily on your own. Even though you might stay within the same occupation, various jobs require various values. If you value working with others, a job with a lot of autonomy is probably not going to fit well with your values.

If you are having difficulty coming up with some workplace values then here is a list of a few to get you started:

- Achievement
- Recognition
- Independence
- Relationships
- Support
- Autonomy
- Working conditions
- Helping others
- Prestige
- Collaboration
- Job security
- Salary or compensation
- Using your skills or background

- Leadership
- Influence
- Creativity
- Variety
- Challenging
- Opportunities
- Leisure
- Artistic or creative expression

While defining your values is important, you should not isolate them from other factors of your work life, such as your personality, abilities or aptitudes and interests.

How to Find Your Voice at Work and Use It!

For many, speaking up at work can be a challenge. Some very bright, smart, opinionated people with great ideas are left silent due to a fear or an internal battle that is keeping them quiet. People might have their voice at work stifled by intimidation, lack of respect, fear of rejection, fear of confrontation, not wanting to draw attention to themselves, being afraid of looking stupid or that no one will listen to them even if they do try and speak (Scivique, 2010).

Having a voice at work is important because you deserve it! When you share your thoughts with your leadership team or with your colleagues, it shows that you are engaged in your work. It should, as long as you are engaging with a positive voice, bring positive attention your way. You will earn more respect from your colleagues and your management team. Your work will become more stimulating as you become more involved. Furthermore, you learn more! When you become engaged with your work, your leadership team will take notice and you should have access to more opportunities within your workplace. There are a few things that you can do in order to find your voice in the workplace and start using it so others will notice you in a positive way.

In order to find your voice, you need to practice many of the skills needed to become a good communicator. You first need to learn to listen. You need to really listen to what others are saying before speaking up or giving your opinion. You want your contribution to be helpful and not hinder the conversation. Nor do you want to distract or be off-topic. You also need to be selective in what you are saying. If you just spout off your opinion about everything that everyone has to say then they are going to stop listening to you.

You should always be sure that you are picking the right time and place to use your voice. Take note of what is going on around you before you just start to talk about things. If there is high tension in the room, you might want to wait until a different time to speak with someone or ask to have a private conversation instead. If you have something important to say, a noisy room full of people might not be the best place or time.

All business conversations should have a professional tone, with a neutral and non-judgmental language. If you are talking in a tone that is making people feel attacked, then they are likely to shut down and become defensive. Using your polite voice and basic social etiquette can go a long way.

While it would be great if your colleagues and leadership team listened to you just because you are you, that is not a likely scenario. Although you deserve to be heard, sometimes you really need to show people proof. Proof that what you are saying is valid or that is it going to work the way you say it is going to work. Collect data to support your idea and present people with facts whenever possible. Even though you might trust your gut, it is unlikely that others are going to trust in your gut. And overall, avoid being a chatterbox. While it is great to be able to express your opinions and ideas, speak in a clear and concise manner. Give your thoughts a voice and then stop talking. You need to give others time to reflect on what you have said and then ask them for their thoughts and feedback.

Leadership Tips to Inspire a Shared Vision

A shared vision is similar to a goal. It is defined with an end goal in mind in which the team works together on objectives to achieve that vision. Inspiring a shared vision helps employees to see the deeper meaning in their work rather than just doing the daily grind. There are two main things that leaders can do to help inspire a vision of the future; define the vision and bring along others by working toward the vision of the future (Mugavin, 2019).

In order to inspire a vision for the future, look at the past and present goals of the organization and how these can help to inform the vision of the future of the organization. Get your colleagues and team members involved in the process and ask them about their goals and aspirations and how they can fit into the larger organizational goals. Focus on how the team's or organization's shared vision will help them to achieve their individual goals. And don't forget to regularly check in with your team to see how the progress on the shared vision is coming along.

When you are regularly checking in with your team about your shared vision, make sure to reflect on what has worked, what has not worked and what you could do differently.

- How do your colleagues and team members

talk about their vision for the future?
- What are the big picture goals for the team?
- How does each individual person fit into the vision for the future?
- How can I, as a leader, include others to be part of this vision for the future?
- Do we as a team think about the future often enough?

Having a shared vision makes you, as a leader, a visionary.

How to Be a Great Leader and Take Action

We often put leaders up on a pedestal without realizing all the difficult decisions they might have to make. We see leaders as having all of the answers, but what we don't realize is the huge mistakes that they can make and the costly failures they might have made in the past. We often think leadership is effortless and comes naturally to people, when in fact, being a leader is no accident. Leaders need to be prepared and tough when it comes to making decisions (Whalen, 2018). It really doesn't matter what decision you make, there is always going to be someone that is unhappy about it.

Setting the table for success is something that leaders excel at. They get an agreement from their employees, upfront, to be able to hold them accountable. This lets people know in advance that they will be called out if they are not pulling their weight. Leaders that take action don't always treat everyone the same, but they do always treat everyone with respect, even if they don't necessarily deserve it. Leaders are there to help every employee reach their potential but not necessarily to help them get to the top of the organization.

Leaders who take action and get results are always coaching their employees. They need to be able to know how to maximize their time effectively and to the best of their abilities. With coaching others, you need to also have a high level of humility. If, you the leader, does something wrong you need to be the first to admit it and take responsibility for your actions.

In addition, leaders that take action also know the importance of self-improvement, personal and professional development. Being a leader is not a destination but rather a journey. As a leader you affect other people in ways that you may not realize can have a lasting impact. If you don't get enough sleep and are crabby to one of your employees, they might become stressed and mess up something within your project. So, as a leader you need to take care of yourself and realize that your actions and attitude go far beyond just you.

There are so many famous leaders and

innovators that just didn't know how to give up and therefore learned from their past mistakes. There is a famous quote by Thomas Edison, "I have not failed. I've just found 10,000 ways that won't work." This really embodies the concept that people should be able to learn from their mistakes and use that to create a better work environment and build better quality leadership skills.

Great leaders who take action are also empathetic and get their team's input before they make decisions. Employees lose trust in their leadership team when things change and they seemingly have no control over it, such as compensation plans or changes to a project. Including your team in the decision-making process can go a long way in building trust with your team. This way when you do have to make decisions without consulting them first, they will trust in your decision.

A good leader should be able to take action and seek out individuals to give increasing responsibility to. When team members are empowered, they will go above and beyond what they are asked to perform to meet expectations. Leaders also ask for feedback when they take actions. When leaders take action they also need humility in order to gracefully receive criticism from their team members.

Lastly, leaders need to be prepared to take action and then get out of the way! Taking action also means realizing that you don't have all the answers and that some people are better equipped to do certain things than you are.

Chapter Summary

Everyone is captivated by a great leader; someone who is charismatic, who can easily sway people to their point of view and who can awe an audience, leaders that are charismatic are able to influence, persuade and inspire their team members. There are several things that you can do if you want to become a charismatic leader:

- Build a connection with your audience.
- Be trustworthy and uphold your promises.
- Show humility and vulnerability.
- Put your audience at ease.
- Connect with your audience at various levels.
- Maintain a delicate balance between serious and easygoing.
- Be confident without being arrogant.
- Understand that you are not the smartest person in the room.
- Show your strong commitment to your goals and lead by example.
- Be in the trenches with your team and get things done.

When you have become a master communicator, you can communicate with a distinct voice that others will recognize. Make eye contact, shake hands and let others know that you care about the message that you are sending.

Leaders are also well versed in setting goals both for themselves and for their teams. They work on establishing S.M.A.R.T. goals, meaning they are specific, measurable, achievable, results-oriented and timebound. Great leaders are also aware of the different types of goals, the performance and learning.

Great leaders also have clearly defined values and consistently work towards them. It is ideal that you have your values clearly defined before you go out and look for a job, but it is never too late to start defining your values for work now. Common workplace values include achievement, independence, support, autonomy and influence.

For many people, speaking up is challenging. But

just remember that you have a voice and you deserve to be heard. When you voice your concerns it shows that you are engaged with your work and aren't afraid to bring positive attention your way. Before you find your voice, you need to make sure that you are listening, you want to make sure that you are contributing rather than hindering the process. You also have to be selective about the time and the place that you are using your voice. Any and all conversations related to business should have a professional tone and ensure basic social etiquette.

Leaders should also be able to inspire a shared goal. They can do this by getting their colleagues and team members involved in the process. When you are checking in with your team about your shared vision, always make sure that you positively reflect on the work that they have done together.

Finally, great leaders are those that are able to take action without sacrificing their integrity. Being a leader is no easy trip and great leaders don't just happen by accident. Great leaders are always checking in with and coaching their employees to reach their fullest potential.

In the next chapter, I will focus on the most common communication mistakes and how to avoid them.

Chapter Five: The Most Common Communication Mistakes and How to Avoid Them

You should already know that communication is at the core of everything and all relationships. In order to build better communication skills, you should also be aware of the most common mistakes and how to avoid them.

Think about the people that you admire, the great leaders, speakers and entrepreneurs; one thing that most of them have in common is their ability for effective communication. There are many things that you can do to ensure that you are being an effective communicator, making sure that you are listening before you are talking, repeating back to the person what they said in your own words, so on and so forth. But what are the things that you shouldn't do? There are many mistakes that people can make in their communication that can lead to confusion and frustration.

Communication is not a one-size-fits-all approach. When speaking with a group of people, some will understand what you are saying, while others might need further explanation. You can avoid miscommunication with a larger audience by first considering the people you are speaking with and their learning styles. Make your communication strategy one that will appeal to all those you are communicating with.

Another very common communication mistake is a lack of attention to your tone of voice. You might need to adjust your tone of voice based on who you are talking to or the situation you are finding yourself in. Before you start to speak, whether you are in a large group or in a one to one conversation, take a breath and access your tone.

People often think they are effectively communicating if they avoid difficult conversations and situations. This is not true. Everyone faces a conflict at some point in their workplace. However, simply avoiding the conflict does not make it go away. If you need to have a difficult conversation with someone, then prepare for it. Write down a list of clear and positive feedback if you have to and always try and end on a positive note.

Poor communicators often hold back what they are truly thinking about. Being a good communicator is about stating what you need in a tactful manner and still being able to understand the needs of others. A good communicator is able to speak clearly while making their requests known without jeopardizing the relationship with the person they are speaking with.

When someone reacts to a situation rather than responds to it, this also shows poor communication skills. When you react to a situation you show anger, frustration, and might be impulsive. When something happens that you feel the urge to react to, take a deep breath and stop before you do anything. First you must understand the facts of the situation, don't jump to conclusions and make assumptions about the situation.

A very big communication mistake is indulging in gossip. It's unfortunate, but it happens. Gossip can ruin people's reputations and drastically break down trust in relationships. Even gossip that is not intended to hurt others can have devastating consequences. As a trusted and effective communicator you should not give in to gossip and you should leave no room for innuendo or speculation.

Close-minded people can make some very big miscommunication mistakes. Today's work environments are becoming more and more diversified. Don't be close-minded about anyone but rather open your mind and your heart to embrace diversity. Embracing diversity allows you to communicate with people who have a range of diverse experiences and creativity which can ultimately be beneficial.

I mentioned this point previously; you have two ears and one mouth, so you should not be speaking more than you are listening. Unless someone has hired you to give a speech - that is a little different. People often think communication is a one-way street and they do all of the talking and very little listening. Don't be that person! If you want to really understand what is going on to be able to effectively communicate, you need to listen to what is going on. This encourages learning and shows empathy to the person you are communicating with.

Lastly, and probably one of the worst communication mistakes, is when you assume you are being understood. This can cause a miscommunication domino effect. You think you are being understood, you give everyone the go ahead to work on what they need to work on, then it all comes crashing down, but you can't seem to figure out why. You made the mistake by making the assumption that everyone understood what they needed to do. You need to check in with people to ensure that they understood your message rather than assuming that they understood it (Daskal, 2014).

There are many ways that you can be misunderstood and make communication mistakes. However, if you are aware of what they are, you can recognize them and work to avoid them.

Chapter Summary

In order to master the skill of communication, you should also be aware of the potential communication mistakes and how to avoid them. Effective communication is not a one-size-fits-all approach. Here are some of the most common forms of miscommunication:

- Lack of attention to your tone of voice.
- Avoiding rather than facing conflict.
- Not speaking clearly while making a request.
- Jumping to conclusions without getting the facts first.
- Indulging in gossip.
- Being close-minded.
- Speaking more than listening.
- Thinking that someone understands you when they don't.

The next chapter will focus on expert tips and tricks for effective communication in the workplace.

Chapter Six: Expert Tips and Tricks for Effective Communication in The Workplace

Now that you are aware of all the mistakes that you can make when communicating, how can you become an expert communicator? When you can effectively communicate with your team members and with your leadership team, you will help to eliminate any misunderstandings and encourage a healthy and peaceful work environment (Belonwu, 2018).

We communicate every day and in many ways. However, being able to effectively communicate at work takes some additional finesse (Watson, 2019). You need to be able to shut off your mind and not think about what you are going to say next but rather fully listen to your colleagues and choose the right words and tone to respond with. The repercussions of miscommunication in the workplace can be far more serious; resulting in loss of employee motivation, poor productivity and an overall breakdown in communication among team members. Here are nine expert tips and tricks for effective communication in the workplace.

First, you need to be diplomatic when you handle conflicts. Conflict can easily arise when people are working together all day long and working against deadlines. Conflicts can result from silly things like someone not changing the printer ink, or from major things like taking credit for someone else's work. Even small and minor issues can turn into much larger disputes. In order to prevent smaller issues from developing into larger issues, get control of them right away. Encourage employees on your team to come to you and let them know that your door is always open. Make sure that you are creating an environment that is comfortable and makes your employees feel safe by ensuring confidentiality. Being diplomatic about the conflict means keeping an open mind and not being judgmental. You are not attacking people or placing blame on anyone but rather asking questions to get to the bottom of things. You should be able to find a solution that is acceptable for everyone.

There are too many conversations that take place

in companies that are a result of email or other technologies. Emails and instant messages are sent to colleagues that you are sitting right next to with a simple cubicle wall in between. Don't forget the art of the simple conversation. Stop relying on your computer so much and resurrect the art of the conversation. While the technology that we use can be very beneficial in speeding up your communications, it can lose its real communicative effect. You also lose out on the non-verbal cues of the communication such as tone and body language. Miscommunications can increase even more when the sender or the receiver of the message does not take their time or is not articulate.

Effective communicators are able to respect cultural differences when they are communicating with others in the workplace. Simple hand symbols or gestures that might be harmless to some cultures could be extremely offensive to other cultures. Many companies hire employees that come from different cultures to work directly in their offices or virtually. As a result, team members and management teams need to be aware of the cultural sensitivities. These can be subtle differences, such as words and gestures, or very blatant differences. The company itself needs to create an environment that is conducive to cultural inclusivity. This can include things like offering specific types of foods in the cafeteria, allowing days off for certain religious holidays and providing training to other employees about being culturally sensitive.

Those individuals that are effective communicators are able to provide good feedback to their employees and team members. Whether you are a leader or a colleague, it is important to let your colleagues know that they are doing well. It increases motivation when an employee's efforts are recognized. Holding regular meetings is a great way to provide employees with feedback, but you don't need to save your feedback and encouragement just for meetings. You can send them a quick email, text or give them a quick call to get a status report and give them your feedback. Ensure that your feedback is clear and concise and that you're able to offer a solution to any difficulties that they might be struggling with (Watson, 2019).

You need to trust in your people! Being a micromanager is not fun for anyone. When you micromanage your employees they lose motivation because they then feel like they can't do anything right when you are consistently hovering over them. As a leader you hired competent employees that should be able to own their own work. As an effective communicator you should be able to communicate to your employees what they need to do and just periodically check in to make sure they don't need your assistance.

Companies that are built on trust actually listen to their employees. When employees are communicated with and feel like owners they will have a higher emotional stake in the company. Transparency is a critical part of the employees taking ownership of the company and their projects. There are very few companies that truly practice transparency and reveal things like their costs and profits. When employees really feel that they are part of the company and that they are part owners, they are more committed and produce more results.

Leaders and employees who can effectively communicate are able to take their emotions out of the communication equation. It can be difficult to professionally communicate in the workplace when there are clashing personalities that you work with. It's unfortunate, but it happens; an argument at work can quickly turn into a personal attack. Before you escalate a situation by reacting to it, stop, take a breath and count down from ten if you need to, then calmly respond without being emotional about it. Don't take other people's reactions personally. Use your "I" statements and don't place blame on others, rather give them suggestions. Be sure that the person you are communicating with is understanding what you are communicating to them and not taking something in the wrong way. Ask them for clarification or feedback on what you talked about together.

Great communicators ensure that they are fully listening when in a conversation rather than just hearing what the other person is saying. It happens to the best of us and that is ok. You are speaking with someone and before you know it, they have had a whole conversation with you and you have no idea what you talked about. Make sure as an effective communicator, that you are actually listening to what the person is saying. Actually listening to someone is much more difficult than it sounds. If you are having difficulty effectively listening in a conversation, pretend you will be tested on what was said. Make a checklist in your head that focuses on the important points in the conversation then recall those points after the conversation has ended. You can also repeat back to the person what they said in your own words to ensure that you have accurately heard what they have said.

Lastly, ensure that your work environment is fun (Watson, 2019)! This might sound a little weird to talk about having fun when talking about communication, however, the two are interconnected. When companies give employees the chance to have fun, they are communicating to them that they appreciate their hard work and efforts.

Chapter Summary

Once you have become aware of all of the various ways you can ineffectively communicate with someone in the workplace, it's time to focus on all of the ways you can effectively communicate with people.

- Shut off your mind and focus on the conversation at hand.
- Be diplomatic when handling conflict.
- Minimize the use of technology in conversations.
- Respect cultural differences.
- Provide good and positive feedback to employees and colleagues.
- Trust in your people.
- Take emotion out of the communication equation.
- Use your "I" statements.
- Ensure everyone is having fun!

Finally, in the bonus chapter we will discuss how to become a master at public speaking and why you need this skill to be effective in the workplace.

Bonus Chapter: How to Become a Master at Public Speaking

Now, you might be wondering why a book on effective communication in the workplace would have a chapter on how to become a master at public speaking. Even if you are not a "public speaker," public speaking is a skill that anyone can master. Many, many people are afraid of public speaking and are therefore not very good at it. It doesn't really matter if you are speaking to a group of investors or just a room full of your colleagues, mastering public speaking can be a big key to success. Learning to give a good presentation is a coachable skill that anyone can learn. With that in mind, let's take a look at how to become a master of public speaking, even if the thought of it currently makes you feel like throwing up.

The very first step is to not get too technical. You really have to consider the audience that you are speaking to. While you might be an expert in quantum mechanics, your audience might not be as well versed in all the technical nuances. Your speech or conversation should start where your audience is (Kapla, 2016), not where you are. If you are giving a speech or having a conversation, think of it like a journey. Where is your audience starting at? How did they get there? Where do you want to take them? And how will you get there?

One key factor to a great presentation is to brighten someone's day or to leave them with something. You should be able to give your audience something that they can take away from the conversation or speech. This can be some actionable advice or a feeling or confidence. Before you start your speech or conversation, think about ways that you can improve your audience's day and go from there.

Something that people greatly underestimate is the importance of practice when public speaking. Once you figure out what you want to say, you need to figure out how you are going to say it. There are three main ways to deliver a speech; you can write it down and read a script, summarize your main ideas into bullet points or memorize the entire thing. While reading from a script can be very effective in delivering your message, it is not so great for your audience. People can tell when you are reading from a script and quickly become disinterested. Your best bet is to memorize your entire speech. If you practice, practice, practice, you should be able to memorize your speech with only having to occasionally look at your notes and be able to deliver a speech that keeps your audience engaged and keeps you in the flow.

Be highly aware of your body language. When people first begin public speaking, they are very often unaware of what to do with their bodies, which can lead to unnecessary fidgeting and body movements. Learning the skill of public speaking is like taking baby steps to work towards becoming a professional. When you are speaking you should be standing still and just using your hand gestures to emphasize your points rather than shifting your weight from side to side or swaying. You also need to ensure that you are taking out your filter words; "like," "um," and "ya' know," are some of the most commonly used.

With great public speaking, less is more. While using slides or other multimedia can help to get your point across or further explain complex subjects, your slides should not be used as a substitute for your bulleted notes. Furthermore, do not read from your slides and put the same information in your slides that you are saying - that is redundant, your audience can read.

Great public speakers are always honing their craft and welcome feedback and constructive criticism (Kaplan, 2016). While you are practicing your speech, ask your friends or family for feedback. You might be surprised at what you learn. You can also film yourself to study your body language, tone of voice and cadence when speaking.

With any speech, it should not only give your

audience something, but also give your listeners a reason to care. Your speech or conversation should not be all about you but rather the speech should be thought of as a two-way conversation. Is what you are talking about something you would like to hear about? If you are having this conversation or pitching something to someone, don't do a hard sell. If what you are selling is of value to the person, they will naturally want to buy from you.

We each have two different voices; our best voice which is our most confident, and our insecure voice. Our insecure voice tends to come out when we are talking about things we are not very sure or confident about. These might be things that we have little knowledge in or that we are not confident in having the answer to. Your best voice is your most confident voice. It might be where you find humor in things or when you are speaking about a subject that you are very passionate and knowledgeable about. With your best voice you light up and could talk forever about a subject.

You must also consider your style of speaking when speaking with others (Lear, 2019). Public speaking skills that you learn can be used either in a group setting, such as a large presentation, or in small and intimate settings like a one-on-one sales call. You can either stay true to your style of speaking, which might be calm and collected or excited and full of energy, or you might match the other person's style of speaking. Some people become very overwhelmed when they are speaking with someone on the phone and they are speaking very fast and are full of energy while other people might then come to up to that level and match their excitement. This is one of those situations where you really have to read your audience and determine what is going to get you the best results.

If public speaking is a skill that you truly want to master, then you need to practice and put in the work. The first big step is practicing; practice in front of the mirror, in front of a camera or in front of a small audience. Practice, practice, practice. Tony Robbins is Tony Robbins for a reason. You can even hire a speaking coach if necessary (Lear, 2016). You are only going to become better at public speaking with practice and input from others.

Chapter Summary

Public speaking is a skill that many should master but very few do. While it can take a lifetime to truly master everything you need to become a great public speaker, there are certainly things that you can work on now to improve your public speaking skills.

- Don't get too technical with niche phrases that only other experts will understand.
- Make sure to leave your audience with something that will brighten their day.
- Practice, practice, practice!
- Be highly aware of your body language.
- Less is more, don't rely on multimedia to get your points across.
- Be welcoming of constructive criticism and feedback.
- Give your audience a reason to care.
- Use your confident voice.
- Be willing to adjust your style of public speaking based on your audience.

Public speaking is an art and a skill that needs to be honed. If you truly want to become a great public speaker, you need to practice as much as you can and in front of whoever you can.

Final Words

Learning how to effectively communicate in the workplace can be a tricky thing, but if done right it can be incredibly powerful. Effective workplace communication takes place through interpersonal communications which are then broken down into verbal and non-verbal communications. In order to truly be an effective communicator, you need to be cognisant of the differences in individual communication styles and any potential barriers to effective communication.

Barriers to effective communication can include anything from interruptions, inattentive listening, a misinterpretation of body language, gender difference, jumping to conclusions and premature reactions to others. Our brains all respond differently to different stimuli as we process through different emotions. When an employee is experiencing stress in the workplace their brains cannot tell if the stress (threat) is real or perceived. This then reacts with the prefrontal cortex and slows down productivity, processing and reasoning, which makes it very difficult to work.

Effective communication in the workplace helps to create a healthy work environment, removes cultural barriers, increases bottom line profits, lessens conflicts, increases employee engagement and productivity, fosters teamwork, promotes innovation, increases employee retention and boosts overall customer satisfaction.

There are many barriers to effective communication in the workplace. These can include, but are not limited to, gender and/or cultural barriers, tone and body language, your emotions taking over, external and internal noise and so on. It is also very important that you keep a positive mindset while in the workplace. Positivity in the workplace has been tied to every measurable aspect of success, which includes profits, productivity and satisfaction. Both employees and employers can benefit from positivity in the workplace.

Good and effective communication also has the power to truly transform a workplace. Effective communication can result in mitigating conflict, increasing employee engagement, creating better client relationships and a more productive and talented workforce. Keep in mind that about 70% of mistakes in businesses are due to a lack of effective communication (Allen, 2019).

Developing a communication style that includes persuasive communication can really take your communication skills to the next level. Your verbal and non-verbal body language, as well as your facial expressions, can play a very large role in how persuasive and influential you are in the workplace. Learning persuasive communication techniques can benefit you in persuading your team members and your company as a whole to change for the better. You need to ensure that you are sending the correct message to your audience with both your verbal and non verbal communication. While you might experience both formal and informal forms of communication at work, it is beneficial to stick to the more formal forms of communication in the workplace.

There are also many different ways that you can use your body language to communicate to your coworkers; making eye contact, your posture, where and how you place your arms while talking or listening are all ways that you non-verbally communicate with your colleagues.

Make sure that you are maintaining eye contact while speaking with people, keeping your posture erect and not crossing your arms in front of you while speaking with someone. Let others know that you are aware of their body language as well and try to encourage them to use positive non-verbal communication.

Non-verbal communication also includes facial expressions. If your face is always tense, people will perceive you as being unlikable. If your facial expressions are always pleasant and soft, you will be perceived as much more likable.

Some of the keys to becoming a better listener at work are:

- Repeating back to the person what they said in your own words.
- Actually listen to what someone else is saying rather than trying to think of what to

say next.
- Listen as though you will have to recall the information later on.
- Maintain eye contact with the person you are speaking with.
- Cut out as much distractions and noise as possible.
- Be prepared to listen.
- Be aware of diversity in the workplace.

Being an effective communicator also means that you can be persuasive when you need to be. Being persuasive and having an influence in the workplace means being likable, having social proof, being consistent, practicing scarcity, having authority and practicing reciprocity.

In addition, effective workplace communicators are also able to give and receive positive criticism. Don't let people giving you feedback hinder your self-esteem or derail your work.

Constructive criticism is meant to help you to grow and become a better employee. You must also learn to give self-critique.

It is inevitable that you will run into difficult situations or difficult people in the workplace. It is how you handle them that makes all the difference. Don't go running off to your boss or human resources right away, try and handle the person or situation on your own in a tactful manner first. If your tactics are unsuccessful, then get leadership involved. This holds true for both coworkers or difficult bosses. Ensure that you are encouraging coworkers to utilize effective communication skills as well.

Being an effective leader is all about having charisma and honing your skills as an effective communicator. Effective and charismatic leaders are able to build a connection with their audience, be trustworthy, show humility and vulnerability, exude confidence and maintain a delicate balance between being too serious and being too easygoing and casual. In order to become a master at communicating, you also must use your distinct voice and portray confidence. Effective leaders are also great at goal setting and are able to get their team on board using S.M.A.R.T. goals.

Some of the most common communication mistakes that can jeopardize all of the effective tactics that you have built up are not paying attention to your non-verbal cues, avoiding conflict, jumping to conclusions, being too close-minded and speaking more than you are listening.

Once you have become aware of the tactics that make communication ineffective, it's time to start harnessing the strategies that will make you an effective communicator. Effective communicators are diplomatic, respect cultural differences, trust in their people, use "I" statements and provide positive feedback to their colleagues and employees.

Lastly, mastering the skill of public speaking can be very advantageous to your career. Many people avoid public speaking out of fear. Here are a few tactics that you can use to master the skill of public speaking:

- Leave out the technical jargon.
- Leave your audience with something to brighten their day.
- Practice!
- Be aware of your body language.
- Don't rely too much on multimedia.
- Give your audience a reason to care.
- Use your confident voice.

With all of these tactics at your disposal, you are

sure to become a master at effective communication in the workplace in no time!

Resources

Adams, J. (2019). *5 Ways to Become a Master Communicator - Tap Inspect*. [online] . Available at: https://www.tapinspect.com/5-ways-to-become-a-master-communicator/ [Accessed 23 Jun. 2019].

Allan, L. (2019). *Poor Workplace Communication Costs*. [online] Businessperform.com. Available at: http://www.businessperform.com/workplace-communication/poor-communication-costs.html [Accessed 23 Jun. 2019].

Belonwu, V. (2018). *20 Ways to Communicate Effectively With Your Team - Small Business Trends*. [online] Small Business Trends. Available at: https://smallbiztrends.com/2013/11/20-ways-to-communicate-effectively-in-the-workplace.html [Accessed 24 Jun. 2019].

Bosworth, P. (2019, February 13). The Power of Good Communication in the Workplace | Leadership Choice. Retrieved June 10, 2019, from https://leadershipchoice.com/power-good-communication-workplace/

Chadwick, P. (2014). *How the brain responds to feedback - IEDP.* [online] Iedp.com. Available at: https://www.iedp.com/articles/how-the-brain-responds-to-feedback/ [Accessed 24 Jun. 2019].

Cooley, A. (2019). *10 Ways Employees Can Be More Proactive At Work.* [online] Work It Daily. Available at: https://www.workitdaily.com/be-more-proactive-work [Accessed 23 Jun. 2019].

Dabbah, M. (2018, May 17). 3 Examples of Cultural Differences in the Workplace. Retrieved June 9, 2019, from https://redshoemovement.com/examples-of-cultural-differences-in-the-workplace/

Daskal, L. (2014). *Communication Mistakes to Avoid at All Costs.* [online] Inc.com. Available at: https://www.inc.com/lolly-daskal/common-communication-mistakes-to-avoid.html [Accessed 24

Jun. 2019].

Daskal, L. (2019). *7 Ways to Be a More Effective Leader - Lolly Daskal | Leadership*. [online] Lolly Daskal. Available at: https://www.lollydaskal.com/leadership/7-ways-to-be-a-more-effective-leader/ [Accessed 23 Jun. 2019].

Daum, K. (2019). *How to Give (and Receive) Positive Criticism*. [online] Inc.com. Available at: https://www.inc.com/kevin-daum/how-to-give-and-recieve-positive-criticism.html [Accessed 24 Jun. 2019].

Dean, J. (2010). *How to Influence People - PsyBlog*. [online] PsyBlog. Available at: https://www.spring.org.uk/2010/07/3-universal-goals-to-influence-people.php [Accessed 26 Jun. 2019].

Dean, J. (2019). *20 Simple Steps to the Perfect Persuasive Message - PsyBlog*. [online] PsyBlog. Available at:

https://www.spring.org.uk/2010/12/20-simple-steps-to-the-perfect-persuasive-message.php [Accessed 25 Jun. 2019].

Edberg, H. (2019). *How to Become a Better Listener: 10 Simple Tips*. [online] Positivityblog.com. Available at: https://www.positivityblog.com/better-listener/ [Accessed 25 Jun. 2019].

Effectivecommunicationadvice.com. (2019). *Barriers to Effective Communication*. [online] Available at: http://effectivecommunicationadvice.com/barriers [Accessed 22 Jun. 2019].

Frost, S. (2019). *How Body Language Is Used in the Workplace*. [online] Smallbusiness.chron.com. Available at: https://smallbusiness.chron.com/body-language-used-workplace-11773.html [Accessed 25 Jun. 2019].

Galek, C. (2019). *How to Protect Yourself from People Who Waste Your Time*. [online] Inc.com. Available at: https://www.inc.com/candicegalek/how-to-manage-your-time-stop-others-from-wasting-it.html [Accessed 23 Jun. 2019].

Grace, B. (2018). *How To Ask Questions That Get Results: #5 Hot Tips To 1,000X Your Results.* [online] Noteworthy - The Journal Blog. Available at: https://blog.usejournal.com/5-ways-to-ask-better-questions-thatll-have-you-solving-problems-smarter-and-faster-af872398fc28?gi=87a0f12c5f2c [Accessed 26 Jun. 2019].

Giang, V. (2012). *17 Tips On Becoming A Charismatic Leader.* [online] Business Insider. Available at: https://www.businessinsider.com/17-things-you-need-to-know-if-you-want-to-be-a-charismatic-leader-2012-1#make-people-feel-like-theyre-the-most-intelligent-impressive-and-fascinating-person-in-the-room-2 [Accessed 23 Jun. 2019].

Giang, V. (2019). *17 Tips On Becoming A Charismatic Leader.* [online] Business Insider. Available at: https://www.businessinsider.com/17-

things-you-need-to-know-if-you-want-to-be-a-charismatic-leader-2012-1 [Accessed 23 Jun. 2019].

Gottfried, S. (2018). *The Body Language Mistakes You Don't Realize You're Making at Work*. [online] Time. Available at: https://time.com/5321644/body-language-mistakes-work-experts/ [Accessed 25 Jun. 2019].

Heathfield, S. (2019). *Dealing With Difficult People Is a Must for Your Career Success*. [online] The Balance Careers. Available at: https://www.thebalancecareers.com/how-to-deal-with-difficult-people-at-work-1919377 [Accessed 26 Jun. 2019].

Heathfield, S. (2019). *Use These Ideas to Know How to Deal With Your Difficult Boss*. [online] The Balance Careers. Available at: https://www.thebalancecareers.com/how-to-deal-with-difficult-bosses-1917887 [Accessed 23 Jun. 2019].

Jenkins, P. (2018). *How Understanding Body Language Can Help You.* [video] Available at: https://www.youtube.com/watch?v=9aWFOK46eqA [Accessed 28 Jun. 2019].

Jenkins, P. (2018). *Importance Of Positivity In The Workplace* [YouTube]. Retrieved June 9, 2019, Available at: https://www.youtube.com/watch?v=AbzJNSIJPbk [Accessed 9 Jun 2019].

Kaplan, E. (2016). *How to Become a Master at Public Speaking, According to The Guy Who Runs TED Talks.* [online] Medium. Available at: https://medium.com/the-mission/how-to-become-a-master-at-public-speaking-according-to-the-guy-who-runs-ted-talks-d65433eb057d [Accessed 24 Jun. 2019].

Lear, K. (2019). *How To Become A Master At Public Speaking.* [online] Vunela. Available at: https://vunela.com/how-to-become-a-master-at-public-speaking/ [Accessed 24 Jun. 2019].

Miglani, B., Ivankovich, M., James, R. and Rodarte, C. (2019). *3 Tips on How to Deal With Difficult Work Situations*. [online] Embrace The Chaos. Available at: https://www.embracethechaos.com/2013/11/3-tips-on-how-to-deal-with-difficult-work-situations/ [Accessed 23 Jun. 2019].

Moawad, H. (2017). *How the Brain Processes Emotions*. [online] Neurology Times. Available at: https://www.neurologytimes.com/blog/how-brain-processes-emotions [Accessed 28 Jun. 2019].

Mugavin, B. (2019). *4 Leadership Tips to Inspire a Shared Vision*. [online] Flashpointleadership.com. Available at: https://www.flashpointleadership.com/blog/leadership-tips-inspire-a-shared-vision [Accessed 23 Jun. 2019].

Page, M. (2019). *The importance of good communication in the workplace | Michael Page UK*. [online] Michael Page. Available at: https://www.michaelpage.co.uk/advice/managemen

t-advice/development-and-retention/importance-good-communication-workplace [Accessed 25 Jun. 2019].

Peck, D. (2017). *5 Leadership Goal Setting Tips for Making 2018 a Success*. [online] Huffpost.com. Available at: https://www.huffpost.com/entry/5-leadership-goal-setting-tips-for-making-2018-a-success_b_5a26c653e4b0f7f1679a0368 [Accessed 23 Jun. 2019].

Petersen, L. (2019). *The Importance of Good Writing Skills in the Workplace*. [online] Smallbusiness.chron.com. Available at: https://smallbusiness.chron.com/importance-good-writing-skills-workplace-10931.html [Accessed 26 Jun. 2019].

Redmond, R. (2018). *How to Report Status on a Project*. [online] Project Smart. Available at: https://www.projectsmart.co.uk/how-to-report-status-on-a-project.php [Accessed 26 Jun. 2019].

Richason IV, O. (2017). *What is Effective Workplace Communication?*. [online] Smallbusiness.chron.com. Available at: https://smallbusiness.chron.com/effective-workplace-communication-822.html [Accessed 25 Jun. 2019].

Rosenberg McKay, D. (2018). *Why You Must Identify Your Work Values If You Want Job Satisfaction*. [online] The Balance Careers. Available at: https://www.thebalancecareers.com/identifying-your-work-values-526174 [Accessed 23 Jun. 2019].

Russell, M. (2015). *How your facial expressions at work could be hurting your career*. [online] Business Insider. Available at: https://www.businessinsider.com/your-facial-expressions-at-work-could-be-hurting-your-career-2015-4?international=true&r=US&IR=T [Accessed 25 Jun. 2019].

Surbhi, S. (2018). *Difference Between Verbal and Nonverbal Communication (with Comparison*

Chart) - Key Differences. [online] Key Differences. Available at: https://keydifferences.com/difference-between-verbal-and-non-verbal-communication.html [Accessed 25 Jun. 2019].

Scivicque, C. (2010). *How To Find Your Voice At Work*. [online] Forbes.com. Available at: https://www.forbes.com/sites/work-in-progress/2010/11/08/how-to-find-your-voice-at-work/#7f41541430ba [Accessed 23 Jun. 2019].

Scivicque, C. (2018). *How to be Proactive at Work: A Five Step System*. [online] Eat Your Career. Available at: https://eatyourcareer.com/2010/08/how-be-proactive-at-work-step-system/ [Accessed 25 Jun. 2019].

Stachowiak, D. (2019). *6 Habits to Keep People from Wasting Your Time*. [online] Coaching for Leaders. Available at: https://coachingforleaders.com/6-habits-to-keep-people-from-wasting-your-time/ [Accessed 23 Jun. 2019].

Warner, J. (2019). *The Women's Leadership Gap - Center for American Progress*. [online] Center for American Progress. Available at: https://www.americanprogress.org/issues/women/reports/2017/05/21/432758/womens-leadership-gap/ [Accessed 23 Jun. 2019].

Watson, S. (2019). *10 Tips for Effective Workplace Communication*. [online] HowStuffWorks. Available at: https://money.howstuffworks.com/business/starting-a-job/10-tips-for-effective-workplace-communication.htm [Accessed 24 Jun. 2019].

Webb, C. (2017). *What Are the Two Ways of Communication in the Workplace?*. [online] Smallbusiness.chron.com. Available at: https://smallbusiness.chron.com/two-ways-communication-workplace-10768.html [Accessed 25 Jun. 2019].

Whalen, D. (2018). *13 Powerful Actions Great Leaders Take to Build Great Teams - Medium.*

[online] Medium. Available at: https://medium.com/swlh/13-powerful-actions-great-leaders-take-to-build-great-teams-5990c052059f [Accessed 23 Jun. 2019].

Zambas, J. (2019). *The Importance of Effective Communication in the Workplace.* [online] Careeraddict.com. Available at: https://www.careeraddict.com/the-importance-of-effective-communication-in-the-workplace [Accessed 25 Jun. 2019].

Zenbooth (2019). *Solved: How to Stop Loud, Disruptive Coworkers.* [online] Zenbooth. Available at: https://zenbooth.net/blogs/zenbooth-blog/9-tips-for-dealing-with-loud-disruptive-coworkers [Accessed 25 Jun. 2019].

www.ingramcontent.com/pod-product-compliance
Lightning Source LLC
Chambersburg PA
CBHW031147020426
42333CB00013B/546